The Wilderness Experience

IDRIS KOLADE OYINLADE

authorHOUSE®

AuthorHouse™ UK
1663 Liberty Drive
Bloomington, IN 47403 USA
www.authorhouse.co.uk
Phone: 0800.197.4150

Published by AuthorHouse 05/17/2016

ISBN: 978-1-5246-2835-2 (sc)
ISBN: 978-1-5246-2834-5 (hc)
ISBN: 978-1-5246-2833-8 (e)

Print information available on the last page.

DEDICATION

This book is dedicated to The Holy Spirit, my Mentor and Teacher. I give all the glory to God the Father and God the Son. I could not have done anything without your help.

ACKNOWLEDGEMENTS

I want to acknowledge my parents in the Lord, Pastors Andrew and Yemi Adeleke and Pastors Segun and Lizzy Kingsley who gave me the platform to serve and to express myself.

Thanks to Chika Akinwale for transcribing the message from the tape and whose contribution helped to facilitate the publishing of this book.

Thank you to my personal and administrative secretary, Folashade Joachim, for her useful suggestions. You have served well and heaven will reward you.

The Leadership and the entire family of RCCG City of David Cambridge, your contribution and faith in me and my ministry has enabled us to come this far. May God continue to increase you all in Jesus name. Amen!

Finally, I want to acknowledge my wife, Olayinka, for her many contributions to my life and ministry, and also my children, Deborah Oyinkansola, Isaac Oyindamola, Shalom Oyinkunola, for their support, love and understanding throughout the time spent writing this book.

Thank you all and may God's grace over your lives never diminish and may He raise strategic helpers of destiny for you in Jesus name. Amen.

Contents

INTRODUCTION

*"For God so loved the world that he gave his one
and only Son, that whoever believes in him
shall not perish but have eternal life." - John 3:16*

*"The thief does not come except to steal, and to kill,
and to destroy. I have come that they may have life and
that they may have it more abundantly." - John 10:10*

*"Yet to all who did receive him, to those who
believed in his name, he gave the right to
become children of God."- John 1:12*

These three scriptures reveal the intended nature of Christians. John 1:12 says, ***"Yet to all who did receive him, to those who believed in his name, he gave the right to become children of God"*** therefore, if Christians are really the sons of God, why are they not exhibiting the characteristics of their father? For example, Prince Charles, the son of the Queen of England, would have a constant level of affluence whether he works or not. Being the heir to the throne means that he is entitled to a very generous package from the government and some things are simply made available to him because he is "Prince Charles". The Bible says that as many as received Him, to them He gave power to become the sons of God.

John 3:16 says, *"For God so loved the world that he gave his one and only Son, that whoever believes in him shall not perish but have eternal life."* When you give your life to Jesus Christ, eternal life is awaiting you. John 10:10 says, *"The thief comes only to steal and kill and destroy; I have come that they may have life, and have it abundantly."*

There is a crucial period between being saved (salvation) and the manifestation of this abundant life in Christ. For instance, there is a time period between a prophecy and the performance of that prophecy and also between a vision and a fulfillment of the vision. This 'Period' is what we would be focusing on in the course of this book.

Jesus Christ was not born an ordinary man even though he came as a man. The Holy Spirit was in Jesus Christ since the day that he was born. Jehovah was his father. The Bible says that the Holy Spirit overshadowed Mary, which means that the gene of the Holy Spirit was in Jesus Christ at birth. Jesus Christ was born a Messiah in order to deliver us and save us from our sins and our predicaments.

"For to us a child is born, to us a son is given, and the government will be on his shoulders. And he will be called Wonderful Counsellor, Mighty God, Everlasting Father, Prince of Peace." **Isaiah 9:6.** He was born a mighty counsellor; yet he was led into the wilderness to be tempted of the devil for a period of time. It took 30 years to prepare him for a ministry that would last only 3 ½ years. Those 30 years of his life were very significant and would determine whether he would succeed in God's purpose for his life or not.

Joseph had a dream about his future at the age of 17, but the dream was not fulfilled before he attained the age of 30. The events that took place during that 13 year period and how he managed or reacted to them eventually determined the reality of his dream.

God singled out Abram at the age of 75 and entered into a covenant with him that eventually made him the forerunner of a generation through which the whole earth would be blessed. The child God promised Abraham was not born until he was 100 years old. The examples given all have a commonality; there was a waiting period that was inevitable. The inevitable waiting period is so crucial because the events that took place during this period would determine the duration of the waiting period and the resulting consequence. In the chapters of this book, I would be discussing what this period means, how to shorten the period, the danger of staying too long in this period, what God expects from his people during this period and much more.

It is my earnest prayer that whatever stage you are in life right now would be your lowest point in life in Jesus' name. Amen.

CHAPTER 1

What is a Wilderness?

The LORD said, "I have indeed seen the misery of my people in Egypt. I have heard them crying out because of their slave drivers, and I am concerned about their suffering. So I have come down to rescue them from the hand of the Egyptians and to bring them up out of that land into a good and spacious land, a land flowing with milk and honey—the home of the Canaanites, Hittites, Amorites, Perizzites, Hivites and Jebusites. And now the cry of the Israelites has reached me, and I have seen the way the Egyptians are oppressing them." - Exodus 3:7-9

"The elders of Israel will listen to you. Then you and the elders are to go to the king of Egypt and say to him, 'The LORD, the God of the Hebrews, has met with us. Let us take a three-day journey into the wilderness to offer sacrifices to the LORD our God." - Exodus 3:18

God told the Israelites that He had heard their cry and had seen all that they were going through; He had heard their cry concerning what their task masters had done to them and had seen their torments. He promised to deliver them and take them to a land filled with milk and honey. Jehovah decreed that the time was up for their challenges and the bondage of 430 years was over - no more living in the land of not enough. When God saw that the hearts of his people had returned to him, He decided to deliver them by his mighty hands from those who enslaved them and honor his promise to Abraham. But strangely, Jehovah decided to take them through the wilderness on their way to the Promised Land.

Everybody must pass through one form of wilderness in life before they can arrive at their Promised Land.

Jesus Christ is our greatest example and he had to go through a period of wilderness before he could enter the fulfillment of his God ordained ministry. Reading Luke 4:1-2, I was shocked to learn that it was the Holy Spirit that led him to the wilderness to be tempted of Satan. It says, *"Jesus, full of the Holy Spirit, left the Jordan and was led by the Spirit into the wilderness, where for forty days he was tempted by the devil. He ate nothing during those days, and at the end of them he was hungry."* Therefore, between the time that God gave you that vision and the fulfillment of that vision, there is a 'period'. This period is referred to as the Wilderness Period.

A wilderness therefore, is a period between a prophecy and a performance, a period between a vision and its fulfillment and it is a period of preparation. It is a school to equip us with what lies ahead and also an information-gathering period, a training period, and a passage to the Promised Land.

If you are going through the wilderness in life, the devil may

not have leaded you there. If you ever have a vision that has not been accomplished, if you've given your life to Jesus Christ, if you ever conceived an idea of something good that has not been fulfilled, or you've been given a word of prophecy concerning your life that has never been fulfilled, then one reason for the delay might be that you have to go through a wilderness period. How long you stay in that wilderness is up to you. You are the determining factor not God.

For example, in the book of Luke 4: 1-2, Jesus Christ went into his own wilderness for 40 days and 40 nights being tempted of the devil. The Bible says that there were wild beasts in the wilderness in which Jesus Christ went through, yet he came out of that wilderness after 40 days and 40 nights and was faced with big temptations but overcame the temptations. He was able to overcome the temptation because he had been trained in the wilderness.

If Jesus Christ failed the day the devil told him to turn stone to bread, if he had said, 'yes! I can do it because I have received power to do it' and he went ahead to do it, God would have sent him back to the wilderness because he has not learned his lessons and he wouldn't have been able to function as a messiah. So, 40 days and 40 nights were meant for Jesus, he went in there and did what had to be done and came out. The same thing happened to the Israelites; God's plan for them was to go from their bondage to the Promised Land through the wilderness in 40 days but some things went wrong and the journey of 40 days became 40 years.

This is what is happening to some Christians. Some

people died in the wilderness and never saw the Promised Land even though they were given the promise - a journey of 40 days became a journey of 40 years. Who was the determining factor? The Israelites, not God!

How long you stay in your wilderness is subject to your obedience, your conformity and your adaptability to the instructions of God.

Being able to yield to the instruction of the one who has led you to the wilderness is of utmost importance to you making it out of the wilderness at the appointed time.

CHAPTER 2

What Happens In
A Wilderness?
What Happens In
A Wilderness?

As mentioned in the previous chapter, a wilderness is any period between a vision that you have and the time it comes to fulfilment. Therefore, it is a preparatory, information gathering and training period when God equips you to face what lies ahead.

Contents of a Wilderness Experience

1. A Wilderness is a Place of Sacrifice

In the wilderness period, God teaches you how to make sacrifices because of the journey ahead of you. By the time you enter into your Promised Land, you must know and be acquainted with the process of making sacrifices therefore, if you refuse to learn how to make sacrifices here, you would remain in the wilderness for longer because God is not a waster of success resources. God doesn't want to commit resources into your hands and then 10 years down the lane, you mess everything up. God would need to teach you during this period before that thing comes into your hand so that you can manage it properly.

One of the principles that God must teach you is making sacrifices. We can see a typical example of this in the lives of the Israelites. In Exodus 3:18, the Bible says, *"The elders of Israel will listen to you. Then you and the elders are to go to the king of Egypt and say to him, 'The LORD, the God of the Hebrews, has met with us. Let us take a three-day journey into the wilderness to offer sacrifices to the LORD our God."* and Exodus 5:1 says, *"Afterward Moses and Aaron went to Pharaoh and said, This is what the LORD, the God of Israel, says: 'Let my people go, so that they may hold a festival to me in the wilderness.'"*

God told Moses to tell the Israelites that they must leave where they were then; the land of bondage, and make a three days journey to the wilderness to make a sacrifice unto him. Therefore, one reason for passing through the wilderness must have been to teach them the principle of Sacrifice.

Every sacrifice involves an exchange. To make a sacrifice, you would have to part with something as a means of making that sacrifice. The bigger the sacrifice the more costly it becomes. Parting with what you have in your hand to make sacrifices to God tends to teach dependence and trust in Him. Sacrifice teaches us the principle of divine exchange as would be exampled later in the case of God sacrificing the blood of our Lord Jesus Christ to have man back. God needed to bring about this awareness to the Israelites in the wilderness because it would be very crucial in their future.

2. A Wilderness is a Place of Temptation

"And a voice came from heaven: 'You are my Son, whom I love; with you I am well pleased.' At once the Spirit sent him out into the wilderness." – **Mark 1:11-12**

"Jesus, full of the Holy Spirit, left the Jordan and was led by the Spirit into the wilderness, where for forty days he was tempted by the devil. He ate nothing during those days, and at the end of them he was hungry." - **Luke 4:1-2**

These scriptures talk about how the Holy Spirit led Jesus Christ to the wilderness to be tempted. Why do you need to be tempted in the wilderness? First of all, it is in order to get tested but God's intent behind the test is not so that you would fail, but rather that you would not mess up when you get to the top.

What you don't deal with when you are at your little beginnings would destroy you when you become successful.

For instance, if you have a problem with stealing (are kleptomaniac) and you don't deal with that issue and you somehow scale through all the discipleship phases in the church but you refuse to take up the opportunity to give up that habit of stealing, if you get appointed into the pastoral office, you would have only succeeded in becoming a dignified thief.

You have to be tested and have passed the test before God can commit something greater into your hands. It is possible that one of the reasons why you have not become your own manager is because where you are working at the moment is a wilderness and you need to be tested so that when you become your own manager, you would not have to go through that test again. However, if you refuse to go an extra mile because it is someone else's business and you are saying 'my job is 9-5, I will only do what I can and leave the rest', God may conclude that since you refused to act faithfully, you have messed up in that wilderness test and you can as well remain were you are for the time being.

There is a saying that the way you treat other people's business would reflect the way in which you would treat your own if you ever have one. Why? You would have developed a particular pattern of work and if lazy, gotten used to a faulty method of operation. Even when you own a business, you would have formed and gotten used to your old ways of working and can't break away from it, therefore, God may say, 'I can't give you that business yet - you are in the wilderness and must pass the test if you want to have your own'. You must go through each wilderness phase and pass every test to enjoy true success.

There are some temptations that are not public; these ones exist between you and another temptation - for example, your employer may not know about your company's accountant making a silly mistake of putting some money into your account, yet you may have already given a testimony at church saying, 'I suddenly found some large amount in my account!' The problem is that this kind of temptation is so secret that if you don't tell anybody and the mistake is not discovered, you might think that you have gotten away with it and consequently not repent about it. I was shocked to learn that the Holy Spirit led Jesus Christ to the wilderness to be tempted. Although, we weren't told what kind of temptations he went through in the wilderness, however, we were told of the examination that was put before him after the wilderness experience.

At the entrance of your Promised Land, there would always be an examination but you can only pass that examination when you have passed the test of temptation in the wilderness.

What temptations are you going through that can stop you from getting out of the wilderness of your life? In my home country, every child has to pass a test before they can move up from one class of learning to the other. I remember that there were some people in my school who had been in a class for two years before I got into that same class and were still left behind in the same class until the school released them to go as they could not move on to the next level.

The next level is coming but you cannot go on to it if you have not passed the test in your wilderness. It is a necessity that you must go through the temptation and overcome to get to the next level. It is not a coincidence that anytime you come to the end of a long fast, you are always faced with one temptation or the other. I found out that immediately when I end a long fast, a major temptation usually follows. The unfortunate thing is that if you fail tests, you are back to the beginning. The wilderness is a place of temptation.

3. A Wilderness is a Place of War

In 1Timothy 6:12, the Bible says, *"Fight the good fight of faith, lay hold on eternal life, whereunto thou art also called, and hast professed a good profession before many witnesses."*

We can note that Christians are not exempted from battles as there is a battle at the exodus of bondage. There would be wars in the wilderness, and before you can get out of that wilderness, it has to be won. The wilderness is a place where you fight the good of faith and come out on the other side a success and a victor. If you look at the case of the Israelites in Exodus 17:8, they fought a war in the wilderness, but who led them into the wilderness? Who led you into the wilderness of your life? I dare say, God! If God has led you into any wilderness in life - if you've ever have a vision from God that has not been accomplished or had a word that jumped out to you from the Bible and you know that that word belonged to you but has not found fulfilment in your life, then God has led you into a wilderness.

For every battle that you fight in the wilderness, be assured that God did not lead you into the battle to kill you. Why? Because He led you into that wilderness to strengthen you; He will not leave your side. Do you know what happened to the Israelites? They messed up and then they accused God of taking them out of Egypt with a promise to take them to the Promised Land, and 36 years later, they still found themselves in the wilderness, not moving forward! They continued to grumble against God. They said, 'It is better if we had stayed in Egypt because in Egypt we still had our daily bread, in spite of the task master and the labour, we could still drink water.' Yet, God gave them water, food, and everything that they needed. God made sure that in the wilderness, every need was met because He was the one who led them there.

If you start working towards a desired end whilst in the wilderness and you have not reached your goal, there is an assurance that if you follow the instructions of the One who led you into that wilderness, the battle will not engulf you. He will make sure that He stands by you to guide you and provide for you. For example, the fact that you are not working at the moment and you are still eating, have a place to lay your head and still have a car is enough proof that He is with you. God, who led you into the wilderness, brought you out of your way of doing things. He brought you into His own kingdom, saved and gave you salvation, and would make sure He stands by you. If you are a child of God and you are in the wilderness with a need, that need is sure to be met. If it is not met, two things are wrong: firstly, maybe it is not a need. If it is a need, and you know that it is a need and it is not being met, then maybe you are not taking instructions from the One who led you to the wilderness or you are not doing what he asked you to do. But once you obey the instruction of the One who led you to the wilderness, He will make sure that He provides for you, and would not leave or forsake you. When things are upside down around you, He'd stay by you.

We came from a place where we had no vision, a place where life was messed up, where we didn't know where we were going, a place of sin and death, and we wanted to thrive but we could not because we were under the task master. What we did, we did not have a liking for! But when God took us out of Egypt, he brought us into the wilderness to train us; and in the wilderness where we were being trained; he looked after us.

God is obliged to look after us in the wilderness; if not, there will be a question mark about his love for his people. For example, if I ask a member of the church to accompany me on a trip to America, I am taking him away from his partner, his home and his job. If I left him alone when we got to America, without support or making any arrangements for a place for him to sleep or eat; don't you think I'll be branded as a terrible person? The moment I took him out of his source and comfort, it became my responsibility to take care of him because I asked him to come on the trip with me.

It is the same thing with God. If God picks you out of your miry clay, saves and polishes' you, He would set you free from the hands of the task master, and would say to you 'come and be my son' as John 1:12 says, **"Yet to all who did receive him, to those who believed in his name, he gave the right to become children of God"**. If God says, 'come into the wilderness with me', it becomes His responsibility to take care of you. On that trip to America, I would make sure that every need of the man is met. But if he goes out while on this trip and sees a Bentley car, then comes to me and says "I saw a very nice Bentley, would you buy it for me?" If I refuse his request, have I mistreated him? The answer is NO!

This is my point; when it is a desire, there are some criterions that you have to meet before that desire can be fulfilled. When it is a desire, God would not just grant it, but He would ask some questions to check out your motive and to show you whether granting that desire would kill you or not. If God gives money to some people, it would kill them. Philippians 4:19 says **"And my God will meet all your needs according to the riches of his glory in Christ Jesus."**, he didn't say some of your needs; he said all of your needs. Why? He is the One that led you into that wilderness therefore; whatever it is that you are asking God for, ask yourself this question, "Is this a need?" Differentiate between a need and a want as this would help your prayer life, your approach to God and knowing the difference between a need and a desire. When you can separate the two, then you would know how to hold on to God by his tie (if he does wear a tie) to ask for a need as it is your right to have it. When it is a need, God is bound by His word to do it.

The wilderness is a place of battle and God would win the battle for you. In fact, it is not your battle, it is Gods' battle and you are just a battle axe in his hands (Jeremiah 51:20). It is the warrior that determines how he uses the battle axe, which is why the Bible says that the battle is not yours, it is the Lord's. Once you are in that wilderness, God takes every battle that comes your way as his own battle. It was not Joshua just fighting on the battle field that won the battle for the Israelites when they were fighting the Amalekites in Exodus 17, it was the hand of Moses that was raised up on the mountain that won the battle, which signified that it was God who was fighting the battle not Joshua.

Every battle that you face while you are in the wilderness of life would be fought for you, if God led you there - He's bound to see you through and that's why you are still here today. There are many people who have faced the battle you are facing now and are dead.

In Mosley hospital London, there are some mentally ill people there and a good number of them are Nigerians. If I revealed their names, you would be shocked as they are known names. The brother of one of the patients still writes letters to him, asking him to send money to him, not knowing that he calls himself 'almighty god' in a psychiatric hospital. What am I trying to say? Some people haven't experienced one tenth of the things that you are going through now and yet they have ended up in a psychiatric hospital. The reason why you have been ill- treated, rejected, have experienced terrible things in life and are still intact is because God is with you. He is making sure that you do not die in the battle field. As long as you are following his instructions, you are safe. Don't forget that for you to enter the Promised Land, you must fight battles but God will go ahead of you.

4. A Wilderness is a Place of Appearance

God often appears to individuals going through their wilderness period. He always appears to his people at this crucial period to encourage and instruct them, among many other reasons that would be discussed in later chapters.

When the Israelites were in the wilderness, God appeared and made himself visible to them in the wilderness in Exodus 19:11, *"And be ready by the third day, because on that day the LORD will come down on Mount Sinai in the sight of all the people."* The wilderness is a place of appearance. When you are in the wilderness waiting for that vision to be fulfilled and have not reached your goal, or when that prophecy is yet to be fulfilled, know that it is time to be watchful. Habakkuk 2:1 says, *"I will stand at my watch and station myself on the ramparts; I will look to see what he will say to me, and what answer I am to give to this complaint."* It is time to seek God's face because God would appear to you.

Every leading man in the scripture received a visitation from God in one way or the other. Every apostle of faith talked about in the Bible became relevant because God appeared to them. If God has called you out of dirt, out of your sin and has brought you to his marvellous light, if He has called you in your old age to bring you into his new age, if He pulled you out of your wretched life and brought you to his perfect life then, be rest assured, He would at one point or the other appear to you.

The problem with most Christians is that they think that until they are face-to-face with God, standing in front of them clothe in radiant white, until He appears to them in their dream or show up in their living room or in their bedroom, God has not appeared. No! In fact, this sort of appearance does not happen too often! God can appear through the words in this book.

Anytime the word of God comes to you personalised, it is an appearance.

God appears to you anytime the word is being preached and you say to yourself that 'Pastor is speaking to me'. Anytime the word of God comes to you in a personalised way, just believe that it is God's way of appearing to you for that moment. When God appears, He does not appear to scare you, God appears to direct you and not only that, to assure you that He is still with you.

Have you tried to do something and nothing seems to be working and all of a sudden, you experience a miracle and you say to yourself 'wow! So God is still with me!' For example, one of my spiritual sons was sharing with me how discouraged and dejected he felt and he didn't want to come to church. He had very many things going on in his life but he eventually decided to come to church and he said that when he stepped in to the church, I was already preaching. The word of God came through me to him that God had not forgotten him and that all is well. I did not know what he was going through at the time but when he told me the testimony, he felt so reassured and happy to know that God is still with him and that He cares for him.

I remember anther story that happened to me not too long ago. I needed a personal item one morning and thought I would send one of my sons to get it for me. While I was thinking about that, the Holy Spirit was ministering to him to buy it for me. The next day, as I was sending him a text to help me buy this item, he showed up in my office with it in hand! How did you know I needed this? I asked. He said that the Holy Spirit told him the day before to buy it for me. With this, it is inevitable to feel good that God still loves me and still cares for me in every little way possible.

That was an appearance. When God appears to a person, it is to show him or her that He still cares for them and that He is still with him or her. When others are being killed by something and you are unaffected, then you should know that God is still there for you - It is an appearance as God would always show up in your wilderness

5. A Wilderness is a Place of Sanctification

"And the LORD said unto Moses, Go unto the people, and sanctify them today and tomorrow, and let them wash their clothes" - Exodus 19:10.

One of the reasons why you might spend extra time in the wilderness is your refusal to be sanctified. Until you are sanctified, you might not come out on the other side. If you are still making the same mistakes that you were making over the years, and you expect God to take you to the next level, He may refuse to do so.

If God takes you to the next level before you are sorted, you would mess up the lives of those who are on that next level.

God does not sort people out in the Promised Land he sorts them out in the wilderness before they get to their Promised Land.

Your Promised Land is a place of enjoyment; a land that is filled with milk and honey. If you've not been 'tidied up' before you enter the Promised Land, you may become an Achan. Achan went through the wilderness with the Israelites but his life was not sorted out, so when they crossed over to their land of abundance - a land filled with milk and honey, he became a problem. The wilderness is a place where God sanctifies you. If you want to get to the next level of your career and the pinnacle of your career, you must be sanctified.

You might ask, what is sanctification? Sanctification is the process of separation from your old way of thinking and doing things, by renewing your mind and aligning your ways to the expectations of your maker. Sanctification is a process whereby anyone, even a drug addict, a fornicator or a drunkard becomes a born again Christian and begins to separate himself from such habits. God allows people to go through the wilderness in life in order to completely separate them from their carnal ways. If you refuse to be separated from your old ways, when you get to the Promised Land, you would ruin the life of other people, not just your own life. Achan ruined his own life and the life of the Israelites. Israel had never known defeat in battle because God always went with them to battles and their enemies were afraid of them because the Israelites always won hands down and this brought fear of the people of Israel throughout the region.

My father once told me the story of a war that happened in 1965 between our village and the next town. When the war began, the king of the next town stopped the battle in the middle of the war and withdrew all the warriors from the war front because they were losing the battle. My father said that the warriors from the other town told their king that they saw some strange warriors among their opponent who wore white and were killing their towns' warriors without using any visible weapon. These strange fighters were diabolical and they just stepped on people and killed them! These strange people fighting the war for the village were not deemed ordinary. As long as these strange fighters were fighting for the villagers, they were winning the battle. The warriors told their king that they could recognize two faces among the strange fighters. So the king tricked the elders of our village pretending the war has ended and invited the two known faces to his palace and smartly inquired about their fellow warriors. After finding out their identities, he sent for them and hosted all of them in his palace. While this was going on, the king sent his remaining warriors to the village and killed so many people that they had to do a mass burial for them.

The point here is that each time you find yourself in the wilderness, there is an invisible hand turning things in your favor. The book of Exodus gives an account of the pillar of fire that went before the Israelites at night and the pillar of cloud that stood behind them during the day. These are spiritual matters. Your enemies, who are not necessarily human beings, try to penetrate your life because you are in a wilderness but they could not, because there is an invisible hand working for you and on your behalf and that is the truth. If you are in this wilderness, the invisible hand is working for you and He will not let you down. Unlike the strange fighters in my story, this invisible hand can never be tricked, deceived or arrested. He created the arresters. You cannot become another Jesus that God forsook. It is not possible because there cannot be two Jesus' and God has forsaken one Jesus and that is why He said that He would not forsake you as long as you remain in him. So when you are in that wilderness, learn what you need to learn and as you come out, you would be refreshed in the name of Jesus.

I can assure you that God wants to sanctify you; He wants to remove all those ungodly things from your life so that His invisible hand and eyes can go with you. As long as the strange fighters in my story were still in the village, their enemies could not win the battle against them; so they had to withdraw them before their enemy could win the battle. God wants to withdraw the sin in your life and imprison them so that you can win the battle of your life. There must be a period of sanctification.

6. A Wilderness is a Place of Commandment and Instruction

During this period of sojourning in the wilderness on your way to the Promised Land, God is training you. Every instruction of God that is kept removes obstacles from your way. The wilderness is a place where God gives you instructions on what to do. The 10 commandments in Exodus 20 were given in the wilderness and God was teaching His people how they should live when they get to the Promised Land. If they can't be taught, they are not qualified for the Promised Land.

Some Christians don't have a teachable spirit and God has been trying to teach the same thing for years; faithfulness, diligence, being truthful and the likes are difficult to practice for such. For example, if God has being trying to teach you how to be a giver all this while because he wants to make you a millionaire, if you don't know how to give when you are earning £100, you won't give when you are earning £1000. In Exodus 20, God gave them instructions about how to live life and about what to do and what not to do. God doesn't teach you how to obey instructions in the

19

Promised Land! It doesn't work like that! You would mess up His purpose for your life otherwise. The reason why some Christians are still struggling to enter the purpose of God for their lives is because they refuse to yield to His training.

Perhaps God is calling you to be a pastor but you struggle to come to church every Sunday. If you have not been trained to attend all services when you are not yet a pastor, when you become one and you don't feel like coming to church on Sunday, you will always send an assistant pastor to preach instead. If you have not been trained to diligently study your Bible when you are not yet a pastor, when the time comes, you would bring guest speakers from all over the world and you will still not study.

During one of our leadership training in church some years back, I asked the people to write down their vision. As I was passing by one brother and I saw that his number one vision was to be a church financier. I said to myself, this is the guy I have been looking for and I told him to see me after service. He came to my office after the service and I opened up the database for tithe payers in the church. I was very surprised that the database showed that he had never paid his tithe in the church. I asked him about his job and I found out that he was working but had not being paying his tithe - yet he wanted to be a church financier. It does not work that way! The wilderness is a place where God gives you instruction and tells you about your future – He'd tell you about where He is taking you to and He'd purge you from things that He knows would be obstacles to your future and adds some things to you that He knows would be of benefit to your future.

7. A Wilderness is a Place of Decision Making

In Exodus 32, the Israelites made a golden calf to themselves and they worshiped it while Moses tarried in the presence of the Lord. When Moses came down and saw this, wisdom came upon him and he said let those who want to be on the Lords side come to him and those for the golden calf should go to the other side. That day was a day of decision and it happened in the wilderness.

It is during tough times in your wilderness, when what you expected was not what you saw or bargained for; when you were expecting God to deliver you but He did not at that point in time because He knows what He is doing; then you have to make a decision, on whether to stay in your church or leave? I have heard people who say because their pastor prayed for them the last time and nothing happened, therefore they are going to another church. I am not saying that it is wrong to go to another church if you feel led to do so but I am saying that some people just make a decision because things are not going the way they feel it should so they leave for another church. But to my amazement, almost all the people that leave eventually realise that it is not changing your church that solves the problem, it is changing your own attitude.

Here is another scenario: You work in a hospital as a doctor and God says, "I want you to stop working in a hospital as a doctor. You have passed your test. Now I want you to sell chilled water in Africa." Automatically, you start thinking to yourself, 'God, how can I go from being a doctor to selling chilled water?' However, what you don't know is that God has programmed your chilled water to be the talk of the town or nation, and that within three days of releasing your water everyone would be asking for your brand of water.

The wilderness is a place where you make up your mind to either stay with God or go your own way. This is because the Promised Land is meant for people that God has trained and those who have decided to stay with God. Joshua said, 'As for me and my family, we will serve the Lord'. I was impressed when I read that scripture - The Bible says that the whole generation of Levi stood with Moses and they said we will go with you and we will serve the Lord. It is no wonder that when God was dividing the land to all the twelve tribes of Israel, He did not give anything to the Levites. The Levites asked God why He had not given them a portion of land and God said 'you don't need to have a portion because yours is the eleven portions.' God commanded that the other 11 tribes should give some portion to the Levites. Why? They made a decision that as for the whole Levites, they would follow God.

What decision have you made recently? Don't forget that you are a product of your past decisions. If you fail to make the right decisions now in the wilderness, the resulting consequence may be too much to handle. The decisions you make now in the wilderness would determine how you live in the Promised Land if you ever get there. It is a place of decision and it is my prayer that the Lord would lead you to make the right decisions during this crucial time of your life in the name of Jesus. Amen!

8. A Wilderness is a Place to Worship God

In spite of all the things that you are going through, you are expected by Jehovah to worship him. We would discuss consequently, how the Israelites failed to meet this expectation, and how their praise and worship of their deliverer was circumstantial and conditional and how their forty days became forty years because they failed to understand their time in the wilderness.

"Whenever the people saw the pillar of cloud standing at the entrance to the tent, they all stood and worshiped each at the entrance to their tent." - **Exodus 33:10**

The Israelites worshipped God when they were in the wilderness but their worship was inconsistent. They needed to learn to worship God in both good and bad times, in season and out of season. They needed to be taught to worship God for who He is and not for what they can get from Him. The wilderness environment is peculiar enough to make people who want to see the awesomeness of God, in other to worship him as such. In the wilderness, if you stay with God, He gives you the solution to what is killing others. If not, can you explain why you are still alive despite all that you have gone through? Can you explain why despite the challenges, you are still in church and as committed as ever; Can you explain how you passed that exam despite what you went through; can you explain how you survived that sickness despite the fact that your doctors have written you off; can you explain how your business has not packed up despite the economic crunch; can you explain how you have been able to cope during that drought in your ministry and how you survived the conspiracy that nearly destroyed what has taken you years to build? Or did you ever think you would survive such a financial turmoil that you recently experienced? In all these it was the grace of God that was sufficient for you, so whenever you are in a wilderness, remember it is a time to worship God.

CHAPTER 3

The Wilderness - A Training School

"And has made us to be a kingdom and priests to serve his God and Father—to him be glory and power for ever and ever! Amen." - Revelation 1:6

The Bible passage above says we are priests and kings and the truth is this that you cannot reign if you have not been trained. Do you know what qualifies Prince Charles to reign after the Queen of England if she died today? From birth, Prince Charles has been trained on how to be a king apart from being an heir to the throne. It is practically impossible for the British Monarch to invite me to be the next King of England after the reign of the Queen just because I am a Christian, very anointed and tongue talking. Those are not the prerequisite for that throne. If that miracle happens, there is a strong possibility that I will mess up because I have not been trained to rule as a King of England. There is a strong possibility that I would lack the civility, the etiquette and the discipline that goes with the position.

There is no reigning without training.

Training Received in the Wilderness

1. **You Are Trained About Faith and How to Exercise Faith.** *The LORD hardened the heart of Pharaoh King of Egypt, so that he pursued the Israelites, who were marching out boldly.* ⁹ *The Egyptians—all Pharaoh's horses and chariots, horsemen and troops—pursued the Israelites and overtook them as they camped by the sea near Pi Hahiroth, opposite Baal Zephon.*¹⁰ *As Pharaoh approached, the Israelites looked up, and there were the Egyptians, marching after them. They were terrified and cried out to the LORD.* ¹¹ *They said to Moses, "Was it because there were no graves in Egypt that you brought us to the desert to die? What have you done to us by bringing us out of Egypt?* ¹² *Didn't we say to you in Egypt, 'Leave us alone; let us serve the Egyptians'? It would have been better for us to serve the Egyptians than to die in the desert!"* ¹³ *Moses answered the people, "Do not be afraid. Stand firm and you will see the deliverance the LORD will bring you today. The Egyptians you see today you will never see again.* ¹⁴ *The LORD will fight for you; you need only to be still."* ¹⁵ *Then the LORD said to Moses, "Why are you crying out to me? Tell the Israelites to move on."* - **Exodus 14:8-15**

This passage from the Bible tells of how the Israelites were between Pharaoh and the Red Sea and how they cried unto God. God asked Moses, "Why are you crying onto me? Tell the people to go forward." I can imagine someone ask, 'Go forward to what?' God commanded Moses to go forward into the Red Sea! Perhaps Moses asked, 'God what are you talking about? I know this region, I was a Prince of Egypt and I know the Red Sea, so why are you asking me to tell the people to walk into their death?' God was teaching them faith through this experience because when they get to the Promised Land, the currency would be faith. Therefore, God said, "Tell them to go forward." And after they had gone forward, God said, "Stretch your rod into the sea." And the sea parted. If they had not gone forward, the sea would not have parted. God had to teach them how to walk by faith and not by sight.

2. God Teaches Obedience

He said, "If you listen carefully to the LORD your God and do what is right in his eyes, if you pay attention to his commands and keep all his decrees, I will not bring on you any of the diseases I brought on the Egyptians, for I am the LORD, who heals you." - **Exodus 15:26**

Then the LORD said to Moses, "I will rain down bread from heaven for you. The people are to go out each day and gather enough for that day. In this way I will test them and see whether they will follow my instructions." - **Exodus 16:4**

"Then Moses went up to God, and the LORD called to him from the mountain and said, "This is what you are to say to the descendants of Jacob and what you are to tell the people of Israel: [4] *'You yourselves have seen what I did to Egypt, and how I carried you on eagles' wings and brought you to myself.* [5] *Now if you obey me fully and keep my covenant, then out of all nations you will be my treasured possession. Although the whole earth is mine,* [6] *you will be for me a kingdom of priests and a holy nation.' These are the words you are to speak to the Israelites."* - **Exodus 19:3-6**

Moses did everything just as the LORD commanded him. - **Exodus 40:16**

One of the biggest problems of Israel, very similar to you and I, is disobedience. We know how to obey God but many times only partially. We pick and choose what we obey in the Bible and when it does not suit one, we call it an Old Testament principle or Paul's doctrinal opinion. Someone once told me that tithing is an Old Testament principle. If you must cross over to the Promised Land (and I see you crossing over) and attain the next level and expected status in life and in God, you must learn obedience. The importance of learning obedience cannot be overemphasised.

Let me teach you a principle that would help you. Learn to obey God in the simple things first and let faith grow in you. By the time you start obeying God in the simplest of things, and you see how God reacts to the simplest things, that would encourage you to obey Him in the big things. Some of us don't pay our tithe. This is wrong! If you are earning £500 per week, multiply 500 by 52 weeks and divide by 12 months this equals £2166. This would be your pay package per month and your tithe would be 10% of the total. The government automatically deducts Income Tax and National Insurance contributions from your salary if you live in the UK. By the time you pay your rent or mortgage, other household bills and feed your family (if you are a family person), you may realise that logically, there is no way you can pay tithe. God knows that can be humanly difficult, but Christianity is not about logic but about faith. If you have decided to be a Christian by being born again, I welcome you to the club of illogical thinkers. The common saying is that 'a bird in hand is worth more than two in the bush', but the Bible teaches that it is in your giving that you increase. The scripture says that there is he who scatters and yet increases and there is he who withholds more than required, and is poor. Even when you do not have enough to meet your daily needs, you are expected to pay your tithe; that does not sound logical to a canal mind but spiritually, it is logically real and rewarding. Sometimes, it may not be logical to obey God's instruction but that is what God expects you to do. We would discuss more about disobedience in the later chapters.

3. **God Teaches the Principle of Giving**

The only reason why the United States of America cannot mess with Israel even when Israel disobeys UN resolution is because up till today, God's covenant with the nation of Israel still stands sure. When Iraq did the same, United States of America and her allies bombarded Iraq with sophisticated weapons and overran the whole country. One day, Israel moved against the city of Gaza, they pulled down and destroyed their houses, people died and in fact they put a blockage against a whole Palestine. Nothing could go in or out, no building materials could go in and the people were suffering, yet the world could not do anything about it. Why? God had made up his mind to protect his people. Look at what the Israelites did in the wilderness in Exodus 36:2-6

"Then Moses summoned Bezalel and Oholiab and every skilled person to whom the LORD had given ability and who was willing to come and do the work. [3] They received from Moses all the offerings the Israelites had brought to carry out the work of constructing the sanctuary. And the people continued to bring freewill offerings morning after morning. [4] So all the skilled workers who were doing all the work on the sanctuary left what they were doing [5] and said to Moses, "The people are bringing more than enough for doing the work the LORD commanded to be done." Then Moses gave an order and they sent this word

throughout the camp: "No man or woman is to make anything else as an offering for the sanctuary." And so the people were restrained from bringing more."

God said give me an offering and they gave God the offering until God said stop! He taught them how to give an offering in the wilderness. If they had not learnt how to do that in the wilderness, when they got to the Promised Land, they would not know how to give though they had abundance. Egypt is a land of not enough and wilderness is a place of just enough. Why? God led you to the wilderness to make sure He gives you just enough but the Promised Land is a land of more than enough. If God hasn't taught you how to give when you have just enough in the wilderness, when you have more than enough in the Promised Land, you would not give to God.

Therefore, God had to teach them how to give when they had just enough. The wilderness is a place where God teaches one how to give. If you refuse to learn how to give when you have just enough in the wilderness, you would stay in the land of just enough. God does not waste His resources - If God sees that you have been stingy with the little He has given to you; do you think God would give you more? No! It does not work like that! For example, if your brother has been suffering and you are able to help but you refuse to help, you have not only failed that brother, you have also failed God Himself.

4. **A Wilderness is a Place Where God Teaches Tithing**
   When Israel was in bondage in Egypt, there was nothing like tithing. Who did they have to give tithe to? There was no priest or church, and so there would be no one to pay his or her tithe to? Nobody! Therefore, God had to teach them about tithing when they were in the wilderness, in the

land of just enough. Some of us are waiting until we earn fat salaries like a professor before we start giving. If you don't know how to give or how to tithe when you have just enough in the wilderness, you would find it difficult when you have more than enough and because God knows that, he makes sure he gives you enough to keep you going.

"As the rain and the snow come down from heaven, and do not return to it without watering the earth and making it bud and flourish, so that it yields seed for the sower and bread for the eater." - Isaiah 55:10

God gives bread to the eater because he sees him as an eater; he would never be hungry because to be hungry is to go against the principle of God. The Bible says in Philippians 4:19, *"And my God will meet all your needs according to the riches of his glory in Christ Jesus."* Food is a need; therefore, God would make sure that He supplies all that you need but not always all you want, in surplus too. God would ensure that you are not hungry. He would give you enough to eat, and ensure that you spend less too because as you step into a store, you would realise that sales are on and enjoy reductions! God made it happen that way for you. You could find that a whole chicken is sold for 50p and you'd be able to get enough chicken to your heart's content. God also said that He gives seed to the sower - When God sees you as a seed-sower, one who is ready to impart the life of others and one who takes pleasure in building his house, He'd begin to give you seed to do that – He'd give you not just bread, but something more than bread – a seed.

The Bible says that God gives seed to the sower. He did not say that He gives fruit to the sower because seed would automatically bring forth fruit if it is within the right atmosphere. The more you give, the more God gives back to you. When God sees that you are a seed-sower, He gives you more seed to sow, such that each time you see someone who is hungry and God says give, and you obey or anytime there is a special church project and the pastor says that you should give and you give, you are replenished and your giving capacity increases to allow for more giving and receiving. When God replaces your giving, He does so with a seed because He wants it to produce many fruits, as God makes sure that He does not replace your one for one, but replaces one for much. Luke 6:38 say, *"Give, and it will be given to you. A good measure, pressed down, shaken together and running over, will be poured into your lap. For with the measure you use, it will be measured to you."*

God teaches us to tithe when we are in the wilderness. If you are a student, don't wait until you start working before you start tithing. Start tithing on the little money that your parents or carers are giving you weekly. Learn to do this now in a hard way! You won't die - that I can assure you. I tell my little daughter that anytime she receives money from me or her mum or anybody else for that matter, she should pay her tithe. Learn it now so that when you get to school, or when you start working, it would not be burdensome because it would have already become a way of life. The reason why some of you are struggling is because when you had just enough, you could not even pay your tithe because you were thinking about the bill and everything else.

If you want to have abundance and if you want God to shut the mouth of the caterpillars and the warmongers and everything that is robbing you of your fruitfulness and your abundance, learn now to pay your tithe. God does this with tithe not with offering - It is your tithe that shuts the mouth of the enemy, allows your children to avoid hospital emergencies and unnecessary spending because it speaks for you. Therefore, learn the principles of tithing now while in the wilderness because this is where God teaches his people about tithing.

5. **The Wilderness is a Place of Trusting and Depending on God**

It is in the wilderness that God has to teach you how to trust and depend on Him and not on your pay package or on your husband, wife, employer or the government but to depend on Him. At times, He teaches you not to depend on your certificates or qualification. For example, a close friend of mine who went to Cambridge University had been looking for a job for three years. He could not even get into a teaching job! God was taking him through a route of not depending on his certificate or exposure because of the future He has for him, therefore, he went through a learning curve of trusting God. This friend of mine became a very successful pastor – this explained it all. If you refuse to trust God, you might not go further.

Begin to trust God now if you want to move forward as God wants to take you to the next level but you can't get to the next level if you don't learn to trust and depend on God for everything. Stop depending on people; they would mess you up. I depended so much on my eldest sister because her husband was the youngest bank manager in my home country in those days. One could practically smell money in their house when one went visiting.

I was quite stubborn back then, so on a certain day, I went to their house and didn't meet them at home, but had their house staff open the house for me. I searched the house for a bunch of spare keys that I knew they had till I found them and then tried out the keys one at a time till the right one opened the door to their bedroom. I went into the bedroom and then opened the wardrobe, and I saw a lot of money in brand new notes piled up!

When I was in secondary school, my father was a farmer and not a very rich one; I told my friends that my sister and her husband were my parents because they would come to the village in exotic cars.

This couple were my alpha and omega, they supported me throughout my secondary school and while I was in polytechnic. When I decided to go abroad, they gathered some money and I applied for a British and another European Country's visa but they could not get the United Kingdom visa however, the Swedish visa came through. I went to Sweden, spent all my money and could not still find my feet and then I decided that I wanted to go to the United Kingdom but I knew I didn't have a visa but later discovered that I had a British Airways ticket with a stopover at Heathrow airport to connect my flight back home to Nigeria.

I then decided that during the stop over, I would get into the country and then never go back home, since I have a sister who was my alpha and omega in the United Kingdom. I was given a 24-hour transit visa to cross from Gatwick to Heathrow airport and I ran into town and went to my sisters' house since I already had her address with me. They welcomed me and I told them the whole story of how I ended up at their doorstep and shared my intention of never going back. My sister said, be ready to go back to your country tomorrow. I thought it was a joke, but to my surprise and disappointment, my sister woke me up at

4am to leave for the airport - I doubt if my sister slept at all through the night.

God set it in such a way that I didn't have any of my friends' phone numbers - I don't know how that happened, but it limited my options. My sister drove me back to Heathrow airport and ensured that I was on the plane back home to Nigeria. Here I was thinking of my sister as my alpha and omega, but now, I was disappointed.

It is in the wilderness that God would teach you how to depend on him and trust him. If you refuse to trust in God and acknowledge Him as your 'all in all' in your wilderness, you might not reach your Promised Land.

When I got back to Nigeria, I could not go back home because I threw a very big party in my village before I left for Sweden such that everyone knew that I was going to Sweden and as a result, I found myself stranded between Lagos and Ibadan (Nigeria). It was during that time that I learnt close to three quarters of what I know today about Christianity because since I could not go home, I got stuck in church and began to bury myself in the word of God and began to trust God. When God took me back to the UK, it happened within one week and without an appearance in any Embassy. He did it miraculously. Why? He had taught me in the wilderness how to depend on him.

In the book of Numbers 13, God told Moses to send men out to spy the land of Canaan. What do you think God was trying to do? God was trying to teach them how to trust in him and how to depend on him, whether or not there were giants in the place. I can assure you that not everyone in that land was a giant on spying the land, 10 out of 12 spies claimed to see giants. God wanted to teach them that there may be giants on the way but with me you are able to overcome. However, they did not see it that way and as a result; their journey in the wilderness was prolonged.

In fact, that was the junction for a crossover, the point at which they needed to depend on God to crossover irrespective of what they had seen. Notwithstanding, because of the report of the others that conflicted with the report of Joshua and Caleb, the two remaining spies, they spent extra years in the wilderness. God is teaching you to depend on him, so please trust him.

You are afraid because you don't trust God. The definition of fear is lack of trust in God. Sometimes physical fear makes you keep the light on in your room till you fall asleep because you are afraid. What brought about that fear? It is the lack of trust in God. The Bible says, "I sleep and I wake up because God was with me." If you trust God, lights out at bedtime would not be scary. Even in darkness you would know that no demon could come near you because God is with you.

Therefore, the reason why you are afraid when fear grips your life is your lack of trust in God and it is in the wilderness that God teaches you how to trust him.

6. **The Wilderness Training School - Where God Teaches Thanksgiving**

He teaches you how to give him thanks in everything - 1 Thessalonians 5:18. When it is good, you thank God, when it is bad, you thank God; in any situation, give praise to God. You must understand that it is not always easy to give thanks in the wilderness of life, but God wants you to cultivate the attitude of thanksgiving. A thankful heart is a prayerful life. Thanksgiving is when you voice your gratitude to God. Habakkuk 3: 17-18 says, *"Though the fig tree may not blossom, nor fruit is on the vines; though the labour of the olive may fail, and the fields yield no food; though the flock may be cut off from the fold, and there be no herd in the stalls. Yet I will rejoice in the Lord, I will joy in the God of my salvation. The Lord God is my strength; He will make my feet like deer's feet, and He will make me walk on my high hills."* A heart of thanksgiving is a heart of gratitude. Even when nothing is happening, thank Him anyway. There is this song that is sang in the church; "Count your blessings, name them one by one, count your blessings and see what God has done … and it will surprise you what the Lord has done!"

Daniel in a strange land proved himself more capable than all other presidents and governors for he had great ability and the King began to think of placing him over the entire empire as his administrative officer. The other presidents and governors became jealous and began to search for some fault in the way Daniel handled his affairs but they couldn't find faults or anything to criticize him about. They decided to inform the king to make a decree that no one should request anything or petition to any god or man for thirty days except to the king, if anyone disobeyed, the person would be thrown into the lion's den. Daniel on hearing this decided to go home, that same day, he knelt down as usual with the windows open and prayed for the third time in the day, just as he had always done, giving thanks to his God. His thanksgiving in a dreadful situation helped Daniel to overcome that wilderness quickly, and he became a Prime Minister in a foreign land in the end. Now you can see why the Israelites spent extra 39 years 10 months and 21 days in the wilderness. You must learn how to thank God in all situations, good or bad.

7. **The Wilderness is Where You are Taught How to Pray**
In the wilderness, God teaches you how to pray persistent prayers. There is a story in the Bible in Numbers 27, and each time I read that story, I am amazed. It is the story of the daughters of Zelophehad, the son Hepher. They were the great, great, great grand daughters of Manasseh and Manasseh was one of the sons of Joseph. Whilst in the wilderness, their father died and when it was time to share the land, the daughters of Zelophehad were excluded because they were women. Zelophehad had no sons and the lands were been given to every male child in every tribe of Isreal. These ladies knew that this was not the time to seat but a time to pray and take a stand, asking for that which belonged to them. They went and stood in front of the entrance to the temple, stopping those who wanted to enter the temple. They spoke to Moses and Eleazar the priest saying is it a sin that our father died in the wilderness?

They reminded Moses that their father did not die because of the sin that every other person committed; they told Moses that their father did not die because they revolted against him or God but that he died of a natural cause. "We want our own portion of the land, why should you deny us of our right? They demanded. With their persistence, Moses had to cry out to God. The Bible says, "And the Lord answered Moses saying, "The daughters of Zelophehad were right in their request". It does not matter if their father had died without any son, they should have their inheritance. In fact that changed the law from that day forward, God made a new law that in any linage where there is no male that the inheritance should be given to the female. The law was established that day. Why? Some people were persistent. It is in the wilderness that God teaches you how to have a persistent prayer.

The Bible says concerning Jesus in Mark 1:10-12 that the Holy Spirit led Jesus into the wilderness to be tempted of the devil and in that wilderness, there were wild beasts. What is the purpose of the wild beast? The wild beast is there to scare you to go back to Egypt – which is a test of your faith and trust in God.

That is why God has to teach you to trust and to depend on him. God allowed the wild beasts in the wilderness to teach you to trust and depend on him. The devil who lives in the wild beast is there to scare you to make you run back, pack up Christianity and to forget about the vision and the prophecy over your life.

You were born a star but there is a time between you knowing that you are a star and you becoming the star that you were born to be and that time is called the wilderness. The wild beasts in your wilderness are there to convince you that you are not a star. The wild beasts could also be distractions that would prevent you from reading for an exam or preparing for a project hence reducing your performance. The purpose for this is to make you believe that you can't finish well or that it is too hard for you. There was a wild beast in education which makes people believe that they cannot pass mathematics, physics or chemistry.

In the wilderness there are wild beasts of unemployment, temporal poverty, bad judgement, low self-esteem and lack. Each time the Israelites were faced with a wild beast problem, they complained to God and wished they were back in slavery! What a clouded judgement!

I've got good news for you and that is; no matter the size or magnitude of this wild beast, your security is guaranteed in Christ. God would keep and protect you in the wilderness and your security is guaranteed in the wilderness so that other people might not say a silly word unto him and offend him because of you. That's why God must keep you through that wilderness. Don't forget that there must be a wild beast in the wilderness but security is guaranteed.

In Exodus 13:21, the Bible says *"And the lord went before them by day in a pillar of cloud, to lead them ... and by night in a pillar of fire, to give them light..."*

He gave them cover and protection from their enemies during the day by pillar of cloud, and then at night when they were meant to be afraid, he gave them light so fear would not come into them; to guarantee their security. It is my prayer that God would bring his pillar of cloud to overshadow your life so that you would not see calamity and you would not see frustration. He would beam his light on your career, marriage, academics, business, and calling in Jesus' name.

CHAPTER 4

The Period of Waiting

Between a prophecy and its performance, there's a process; between your salvation and living an abundant life; between your vision and the fulfillment of that vision, there are periods which we call 'the period of the wilderness or of waiting'. There cannot be a promised land without a wilderness, in one way or the other, in order for you to get to that Promise Land, you must go through a wilderness, and it is compulsory. Just like paying a price is for true success, every person on the surface of the earth must go through a wilderness before they can get to their promised land. God designed it that way to make us better people.

We've covered a lot about the wilderness experience; what the wilderness is all about, what happens in the wilderness and finally that the wilderness is a training school. We said that it is in the wilderness that God trains you about faith; obedience; giving; tithing; offering; how to war; the principles of warfare; how to have a persistent prayer; how to trust and depend on Him and how to live a holy and sanctified life so that by the time we get to our Promised Land, our life is not messed up. We went on to say that when we are in the wilderness, there are wild beasts. The purpose of the wild beasts is to scare you to change your course in life and to stop running the race of purpose. The good news is that despite the wild beasts, security is guaranteed in Christ because it was God that led you to the wilderness and He will make sure that you are safe. We also said that in the wilderness, all your needs are met because before the wilderness is the land of 'not enough'. The wilderness is the land of 'just enough' because God has to keep you going and He has to be with you. That's why the problem that you are going through has not overcome you.

If God led you into that wilderness, your need in the wilderness has to be met by Him. However, it is only your need that would be met here. Desires may not be met in the wilderness because they come into fulfillment in our Promised Land. The beauty of an achievement relates to the time of that achievement. It is worthless for a 120-year-old man to win the lottery because he may not even live long enough to enjoy the lottery. Therefore, how long you live or stay in your wilderness is subject to your obedience, your conformity, and your adaptability to the word and the instructions of God. How long you stay in your wilderness is your choice, God is not the determining factor. You yourself are the determining factor. Jesus went into the wilderness of His life for forty days and forty nights and He came out victorious.

When He came out, Jesus was tempted with big temptations, three times and He overcame them. He could overcome them in the wilderness because He had already been trained. I usually pray that what others achieve in ten years, God would give in two years because God did it for me. When I was leaving my home country, I made an offering that was very painful - I was in Nigeria, Africa and made the offering in pounds – which was to facilitate my journey to the UK. I put everything into the offering basket, and as I was dropping it in the offering basket, the man of God said, "Someone has just dropped something and it is painful. God said that you should ask Him for anything." Not thinking about what I said, I just opened my mouth and said, "Father, take me to the UK. What others achieve in ten years, give it to me in two years!" and the Lord did it. Without being proud, within those two years, I bought six flats in a posh area in my country, and got my Indefinite Leave to Remain in the UK, and a lot more.

Therefore, what others are achieving in 20 years, God gave them to me in 2 years! May you never spend extra hours in bondage in the mighty name of Jesus! May you never spend overtime in your wilderness bearing in mind that you have to pass through it, not live in it.

CHAPTER 5

Reasons Why the Journey of 40 Days Became 40 Years

D elay can be very stressful but let's see why the journey of the Israelites were prolonged.

1. They Were Inconsistent

If you want to see people who are inconsistent, take a look at the Israelites. In the book of Exodus, chapters 7 to 12, God did wonderful miracles and they saw these miracles. Two chapters after, in Exodus 14, they came face-to-face with the Red Sea and they messed up. They told Moses, "If you know you can't lead us, please send us back because you have brought us to a place where the Red Sea is in front of us and the Egyptians are behind us and we are stuck in between both". What amazes me is that God did not kill them, instead He opened the Red Sea for them and right after they crossed the Red Sea, they were so impressed with what God did that Moses composed a song and everyone joined in the jubilation and celebration and they danced and rejoiced. Miriam, Moses' sister danced also and said wonderful things about God.

Howbeit, immediately after that celebration, their inconsistency showed. In Exodus 15, they were praising God, and in Exodus 16 they began to grumble against God. When you are in church, you worship God with lifted hands, as soon as the service ends and you leave the church to go home, you begin to play un-churched songs that do not edify God or his spirit within you. When someone steps on your toes outside of church, you flare-up, but if the same thing happens in church, you respond with a 'God bless you' using your most holy voice – a truly inconsistent attitude. For example, a couple believing God for the fruit of the womb and you burst into worship and thanksgiving towards God, singing praises and declaring his faithfulness when they realise that the wife is pregnant. On the day of delivery, when she finds herself in pain, she'd say all sorts of things to God forgetting that He can bring her through the time of labour.

When you get a job, everybody is celebrating and you are excited saying this is your dream job and just three days later, you say this is not the job for you – this shows the inconsistency of man! The Israelites were perpetually inconsistent and it's no wonder that they spent 40 years on a journey of 40 days. When God did a miracle amongst them, they applauded and immediately after, they begun to moan. There is a saying in my home country which when interpreted is this: 'if you want to be hot, be hot, if you want to be cold, be cold, being lukewarm is of no distinction'. For some of you, the wild beast that is chasing you should not even come near you because you have seen God part the Red Sea and you've seen him deal with the Egyptians. Why should providing water for you in the wilderness be a problem to God if He can part the Red Sea? You shouldn't be afraid of whatever it is that is making you fearful because there are a thousand and one things you can be thankful for that God has done for you and God can do this too!

2. Murmuring and Complaining

There is a big difference between murmuring and asking. Murmuring and complaining would make you spend extra time in the wilderness. What does it mean to murmur? The dictionary says to murmur is to mutter something that it is indistinctive, not clear and is cloudy.

What does it mean to complain? To complain means to make a formal accusation or charge. I'm tired of the Church of God murmuring! The Church knows how to murmur, not to ask. We know how to murmur but we don't know how to ask. Sometimes, most of our asking is actually murmuring. We mutter some words and we complain, when we should be asking.

He who murmurs spends extra time in wilderness.

God did miracles for His chosen, the Israelites, when they were in Egypt. During the plague, the firstborns of the Egyptians died, but their own firstborns were spared. They saw God parting the Red Sea yet when faced with thirst and instead of asking, they began to murmur, and complain. The Bible says, 'Israel murmured against Moses'. No wonder they spent extra years in the wilderness.

*22 **Then Moses led Israel from the Red Sea and they went into the Desert of Shur. For three days they travelled in the desert without finding water.** 23 **When they came to Marah, they could not drink its water because it was bitter. (That is why the place is called Marah)** 24 **So the*** *people grumbled against Moses, saying, "What are we to drink?" - Exodus 15:22-24*

In the desert the whole community grumbled against Moses and Aaron. - Exodus 16:2

But the people were thirsty for water there, and they grumbled against Moses. They said, "Why did you bring us up out of Egypt to make us and our children and livestock die of thirst?" - Exodus 17:3

Notice how Israel murmured against Moses. Please brethren, stop murmuring! Most times, Christians waste God's time by murmuring. They just keep on muttering when all they should say is, "God please, give me admission into the university, give me favour." I remember when I came back from boarding school during my secondary school days and all my mates were buying stretched jeans, so I wanted a pair too. I approached my mum, because I couldn't go to my dad, and said, "Mum, all my mates are buying stretched jeans so I need some money to buy one." She said, "What stretched jeans! Get out of here!" And then I started murmuring. I said, "So if you knew you couldn't buy me stretched jeans, why then did you bring me to this world? Did I bring myself to the world? If you knew that you couldn't take care of me, why then did you bring me to the world?" That was my accusation against my mother. That's how bad I was and she reported me to my dad. Don't let me tell you the other part of the story!

Most of the time that is what we do; we murmur and complain like the Israelites. They said, "Moses, you knew we would die of thirst, you knew you could not give us water, why then did you bring us out of Egypt, Why?" Stop murmuring and start asking. Everyone that asks shall receive, not everyone that complains or murmurs. Ask, the Bible says, and it shall be given unto you, not murmur and the food will be delivered to your table. Also, when things seem not to be working, don't complain or make accusations. When there is a sickness that would not leave your body, please don't complain. If you want to speak to God about it, please do but make sure you do so by asking and not murmuring. Christians, if you don't want the journey of one year to become a journey of one hundred years, stop murmuring. Murmuring is so irritating, because you cannot hear what the person is saying.

God wants to hear you. God wants to hear your voice so make it clear. It takes grace for God to give you what you murmur about. If I complimented my mum and helped her around the house (and I am not talking about manipulation) asking if she had anything in the house for me to do, then my mum would have said, "What do you want?" Do you know that and there's a possibility that my mum might have given it to me instead of me laying accusations and making charges against her; I did not get my stretch jeans. In fact, I got some lashes on my butt instead. Please don't murmur. It keeps you longer in the wilderness.

3. Disobedience

"Then the LORD said to Moses, "Look, I'm going to rain down food from heaven for you. Each day the people can go out and pick up as much food as they need for that day. I will test them in this to see whether or not they will follow my instructions." - Exodus 16: 4

Look at the word *"test them."* The King James Version (KJV) says, *"That I may prove them"*. This happened after they complained about food and God gave them food; He gave them manna. God said to Moses, 'I'm going to rain down some manna and with this manna will I test my people if they will obey me'. As a test, God told them to collect appropriate portion for daily use only, and they must not allow any left over to the next day because a fresh portion would be made available for each day.

What are you going through that may be a test? That opportunity you just had may be a test. The money that came to your hand yesterday may be a test. What is it that you are going through right now that may be a test from God? "Let me test them if they will obey me." This is not the test from the devil. This is not temptation from Satan; it's a test from God. It is not a temptation that is aimed at your downfall, but a test that is aimed at your lifting up. It is to take you to the next level. God said, "Let Me test them", yet they began to gather manna until there was nothing else to put more manna into. I could imagine that some people would create an altar in their house and put manna there.

Why did they do that? They did not trust God and God needed to teach them how to trust Him in the wilderness. Some took excess because they were lazy, saying; 'You see, instead of the hassle of going all the time to gather food, let me put everything here so that tomorrow morning when everyone is going to gather some food, I could have a lie in.' For some Christians, it is laziness that would keep them in their wilderness.

God is not a magician, for there to be a performance, there must be a process.

God will not bypass a process of learning for you; you have to go through it. Every woman must carry a baby in her belly for a certain period of time before giving birth, and when she is about to give birth, it is either by natural birth or caesarean, either way she would still feel the pain of childbirth. Even if she is operated on to deliver the baby, 3 days after, she'd still feel the pain. It is not possible to wake up and find the baby that was inside of you by your side without being cut open or giving birth. There must be a process.

Some people are physically lazy. They could still be in bed at 10 am; and usually get to work late. They call their manager and tell a lie; "I am sorry for coming late. I am not feeling too well." For some others, theirs is not physical laziness, it is mental laziness. They can't think. One day, I was very upset with my little boy. He asked me a question, and I replied, "What sort of question is that, can't you think?" He said, "Err, I can't think", and I was so upset that I shouted at him "Think boy! That is what is called mental laziness, don't be lazy". If you are mentally lazy, the journey of one day would become a three-year journey. When other students are busy studying and keeping their legs in cold water so they don't fall asleep, you are deeply asleep. You keep saying, "The exam is still three days away". If a problem occurred two days to your exam, by the time you are done dealing with the problem, you would realise that there is no time to study anymore. Please wake up! Don't forget that the number of problems that you can solve determines your pay package. That means your financial stance in life, goes simultaneously with how much you can use your brain. If you got your first degree, that shouldn't be it. Go back to school. The day you stop learning is the day you start dying. Mental laziness can cause some people extra time in the wilderness. But God can revive your brain if you ask him to. If you are trying hard to achieve something and it's not working, it is understandable. But when you are not trying at all, God would not do a miracle. Use your brain!

Your pay package is subject to how much you can use your brain, how much problem you can solve for others.

One reason why some of the Israelites disobeyed God was because they were just greedy. They'd forgotten that the manna of today turns to maggots tomorrow. So if you have something in your hand that God has given to you as manna to use now and you don't use it or do what God wants you to do with it, it becomes a maggot. In Exodus 16:20, the Bible says, *"But some of them didn't listen and kept some of it until morning. But by then it was full of maggots and had a terrible smell. Moses was very angry with them."*

Do you know some people's houses; their wardrobes and their rooms are full of maggots? If you have clothes, shoes or bags that you have not used in the last six months that may be a maggot. You are not using it because someone else needs it. If you have a car parked there and you've not used it for the past one year, give them out to others who need them because to you it's a maggot but to someone else, it could be manna. In other words, what is maggot to you may be manna to others. But when you buy something and you are using it, it's a blessing; it's something that would make you feel comfortable. The moment you stop using it and you pack it there and someone else needs it and you refuse to give it out, it becomes a maggot in the eyes of God. So your house may be full of maggots and until you get those maggots out of your houses, you may not be able to get out of that wilderness.

After God preached this message to me during my personal study, I went into my wardrobe, gathered some stuff and started giving them out to people. It was then I realised that they were maggots. Some of them were very old suits, they were maggots but when I got rid of those maggots, God began to beautify my life. People were just blessing me with Ted Baker Suits, TM Lewin Suits and shirts etc. The Israelites were disobedient unto God, they were greedy and covetous.

4. They Tempted God

¹ *The whole Israelite community set out from the Desert of Sin, travelling from place to place as the LORD commanded. They camped at Rephidim, but there was no water for the people to drink.* ² *So they quarrelled with Moses and said, "Give us water to drink." Moses replied, "Why do you quarrel with me? Why do you put the LORD to the test?"* ³ *But the people were thirsty for water there and they grumbled against Moses. They said, "Why did you bring us up out of Egypt to make us and our children and livestock die of thirst?"* ⁴ *Then Moses cried out to the LORD, "What am I to do with these people? They are almost ready to stone me."* ⁵ *The LORD answered Moses, "Go out in front of the people. Take with you some of the elders of Israel and take in your hand the staff with which you struck the Nile, and go.* ⁶ *I will stand there before you by the rock at Horeb. Strike the rock, and water will come out of it for the people to drink." So Moses did this in the sight of the elders of Israel.* ⁷ *And he called the place Massah and Meribah because the Israelites quarrelled and because they tested the LORD saying, "Is the LORD among us or not?"* - Exodus 17:1-7

The Bible says that they tempted God. Do you know howmany times you've tempted God? I can hear you say; 'Me, tempt God, never!' Do you know what it means to tempt God? Tempting God is being aware of God's providence, and yet rebels against Him by not trusting Him. It is when you commit a sin on purpose and you say 'what will God do?' Or you say 'let me make a vow and not keep that vow and see what God will do', 'let me slap my wife and see what God will do.'

Do Christians also beat their wives? Well, it is unfortunate, but it does happen. Or you say, 'Let me not pay my tithes and see what God would do.' That is tempting God. Does it sound familiar now? God is still God over the devil and all he represents including sicknesses and diseases, lack and poverty, etc. Can you believe that? He is still the Commander-in-Chief of everything, so please don't tempt

Him! You don't have control over God. He is the one who controls all things. He would only have mercy on whom He will have mercy and compassion on whom He will have compassion. You cannot continue to take him for granted. Paul said in Romans 6:1-2, *"What shall we say, then? Shall we go on sinning so that grace may increase?* [2] *By no means! We are those who have died to sin; how can we live in it any longer?"* So when grace expires on your ill action, the consequence is devastating. Israel tempted God and they spent overtime in the wilderness.

5. Broken Covenants and Promises

Broken covenants can cost you extra time in the wilderness. Let us go through some scriptures to see how the Israelites kept on breaking their covenant with God. Exodus 3:18 (New Living Translation) says, *"The elders of Israel will accept your message. (God speaking to Moses), Then you and the elders must go to the king of Egypt and tell him, 'The LORD, the God of the Hebrews, has met with us. So please let us take a three-day journey into the wilderness to offer sacrifices to the LORD, our God."*

54

And then, Exodus 5:1, 3 (New Living Translation) says, *"After this presentation to Israel's leaders, Moses and Aaron went and spoke to Pharaoh. They told him, "This is what the LORD, the God of Israel, says: Let my people go so they may hold a festival in my honour in the wilderness."" *³ But Aaron and Moses persisted. "The God of the Hebrews has met with us," they declared. "So let us take a three-day journey into the wilderness so we can offer sacrifices to the LORD our God. If we don't, he will kill us with a plague or with the sword."*

In Exodus 3:18, God instructed the Israelites to go into the wilderness and in three days make a sacrifice unto Him. They confessed it over and over again in Exodus 5:1 & 3 when they wanted something from God; when they wanted deliverance from the hand of Pharaoh, they said that God told them to go out of Egypt into the wilderness and in three days make a sacrifice unto Him. Look at the broken covenant; forty-five days after, nobody, not even Moses was talking of the covenant, or offering that they were supposed to have made three days into their wilderness journey. Forty-five days after, nothing happened. In fact, we don't know the actual date that the sacrifice was made, but according to the scripture, the time frame was between forty-five and ninety days. Let us take a look at it.

"Then the whole community of Israel set out from Elim and journeyed into the wilderness of Sin, between Elim and Mount Sinai. They arrived there on the fifteenth day of the second month, one month after leaving the land of Egypt."
- Exodus 16:1

According to the above scripture, fifteen days in the second month makes it forty-five days after which they left Egypt. At that point in time, they had not made the sacrifice that they promised God they would do in three days. Now in Exodus 19:1, it says, *"On the first day of the third month after the Israelites left Egypt—on that very day—they came to the Desert of Sinai."* They got to the Wilderness of Sinai three months after they left the land of Egypt. This made it about 90 days since they left Egypt.

They made this sacrifice in Exodus chapter 18 and it took Jethro, Moses father-in law, to remind Israel and Moses that they needed to make a sacrifice to their God as promised. That happened between forty-five and ninety days since God told them they were going to make a sacrifice in three days. This was a broken covenant and promise.

Let me tell you a story about myself and my experience of a broken promise. When I was leaving my home country for United Kingdom some years back, I asked God for some things and I promised in return to serve him throughout my stay in Diaspora. God answered my prayers and made sure He fulfilled his part of the contract in record time. When I was planning to travel, I prayed; "Father, help me get to the United Kingdom and I will serve you faithfully. Plant me in a vibrant church, where my service to you can be effective."

Everything I asked God for, He did. He got me into the UK miraculously, and within days he planted me in a very vibrant church, few doors from where I was staying. Immediately I stepped into that Church, everybody including the pastor just loved me, it was an answered prayer. Soon after I got settled into the church, I got fed up because they wanted me to get busy - come for prayer meetings, for bible study, night vigil, lead prayer meetings and teach Sunday school. It got to a point that I said to myself, No! No!! No!!! "I came to UK to make money not for all these. I did all these in my country I don't need them now".

I completely ignored my covenant with God. He played His own part of the covenant, but I refused to do mine. I started missing mid-week services and some other meetings and devoted my time to making money but God allowed it, and I made some good money. There was a time when my wife needed to put my clothes into the washing machine and she found £500.00 in the pocket of one of my trousers. I didn't know that I had £500.00 in there. I would take my suit to the dry cleaner, and each time the dry cleaner attendant would give me something that he found in my pocket when I went back for my clothes - I made so much money that I lost track of where I kept them. One day, I said to myself, "Ok. You have made money so what next?" I decided to start a business of exporting X-Ray films to Nigeria. The first set of trips went okay and I made more money, then I became greedy and covetous to the point of exporting a whole container of x-ray films to Nigeria. I lost all of it and realised that I had not kept my own part of the deal - God reminded me and I cried like a baby on that day.

I travelled to Lagos, Nigeria to see what I could do to limit my losses but as I was settling down after a long flight from London at my friend's house (before going to face the reality of what had happened) some men came to visit. Before I knew what was happening, one of them slapped my face! I saw stars and rainbows! One of them said, "We are armed robbers, cooperate!" They took everything, but thank God they didn't touch my passport or kill me, God saved my life. I flew back to London on the third day and asked God, "What is this?" God reminded me, "Son! You broke the covenant! This is not what we agreed, I promised to look after you and I did and you promised to serve me but you never did!"

Broken promises would make a journey of one day to become a journey of a thousand years. Truthfully, I went back to queue again. God is a just God; if I had not learned it, maybe I wouldn't have been a pastor today.

God has to allow some things even if they will have to cause you some temporal discomfort. God is not worried about your temporal shame if the end result will get you to where he wants you to be and bring him glory.

If it's not compulsory for you to work on Sunday and you sacrificed going to Church for work on Sunday, the money you earn that day is greed. If you spend the time you are meant to spend in the presence of God working or doing something else, whatever you get from that thing is greed. Please look out for my book, *"The Blood Money"* as I went into more details about this in it. I never kept my own part of the deal and I learnt my lesson the hard way. In what area are you not keeping your own part of the deal with God or with man?

I told the members of our church in Cambridge, UK (a multi-national congregation) that when some of them were leaving their countries, they made some serious promises to God and entered into some serious covenant with God just because they needed his favour to achieve their aims of going abroad. Some of them entered into these agreements because they were desperate for money or needed God's favour to obtain their travel documents. When they needed God desperately, they knew how to cry unto God. Some of them would say, 'God! If only you could just take me abroad, I would serve you.' The question I asked them was, "Are you serving Him now?" Most of the time, the answer is NO. This is a broken promise. Friends, this may be the reason for your struggle today. God may be calling you to return to your first love for Him.

The Israelites said 'in three days, we would make a sacrifice unto God.' Forty-five days after, they were busy murmuring, complaining, enjoying the goodness of God, enjoying the manna from God, His water from the rock and they forgot their own part of the deal; broken promises. No wonder they spent extra time in the wilderness. Exodus 19:4-6, 7-8 says,

[4] *'You have seen what I did to the Egyptians. You know how I carried you on eagles' wings and brought you to myself.* [5] *Now if you will obey me and keep my covenant, you will be my own special treasure from among all the peoples on earth; for all the earth belongs to me.* [6] *And you will be my kingdom of priests, my holy nation.' This is the message you must give to the people of Israel."*

Everyone has a contract with God and every contract has two sides to it, which is why it is a contract. It is an agreement between two or more parties. In the above scripture, God laid down the contract – "'If you obey me', He said, 'I would keep my covenant.'" And He told them what they should expect from Him.

[7] *So Moses returned from the mountain and called together the elders of the people and told them everything the LORD had commanded him.* [8] *And all the people responded together, "We will do everything the LORD*

has commanded." So Moses brought the people's answer back to the LORD.

They told Moses that everything God asked them to do, they would do. Moses went to feedback this response of the people to God and in chapter 20 in the book of Exodus, God gave the law. God did not give them a law until they committed themselves to obey the law of God. In Exodus 24:3, the Bible says, *"Then Moses went down to the people and repeated all the instructions and regulations the LORD had given him. All the people answered with one voice, "We will do everything the LORD has commanded."* On the delivery of God's expectation to remain in covenant, the people again said, 'we would obey ALL. They told Moses in verse 7 of the same chapter that they would keep their own part of the covenant. ⁷ *Then he took the Book of the Covenant and read it aloud to the people. Again they all responded, "We will do everything the LORD has commanded. We will obey."*

The people solemnly promised to obey every one of the rules but in Exodus 32, Moses went to meet with the LORD on the mountain and he was delayed. Perhaps, he was enjoying his fellowship with God – however, before he came back, the people gathered together and said to each other, in Exodus 32, 'we don't know what has happened to "this Moses"' – their leader was now being referred to as "this Moses"!

"When the people saw that Moses was so long in coming down from the mountain, they gathered around Aaron and said, "Come, make us gods who will go before us. As for this fellow Moses who brought us up out of Egypt, we don't know what has happened to him." - Exodus 32:1

They turned to Aaron and said 'please make us a god to lead us.' They've forgotten that they told God that they would obey all and one of the things that God told them was in the book of Exodus 20: 4, *"You shall not make for yourself an image in the form of anything in heaven above or on the earth beneath or in the waters below."* When Moses gave them this word, they told Moses, we would do ALL.

Consider your ways, think about how many vows you've made in life whether in Church or elsewhere and those you have never kept, do you expect to get out of that wilderness that way? You need mercy because nobody forced you to make the vow. The Bible says in Ecclesiastes 5: 4-7, *"When you make a vow to God, do not delay to fulfil it. He has no pleasure in fools; fulfil your vow.[5] It is better not to make a vow than to make one and not fulfil it.[6] Do not let your mouth lead you into sin. And do not protest to the temple messenger, "My vow was a mistake." Why should God be angry at what you say and destroy the work of your hands?[7] Much dreaming and many words are meaningless. Therefore fear God."*

The day you gave your life to Jesus, and you declared, "Jesus! I accept you as my Lord and my Saviour. Whatever you ask me to do I will do, wherever you lead me, I will go" and Jesus Christ said, "Fine, if you do that then I'll be Your Lord, I'll be your comforter, I'll be your chief Judge, and I'll be your advocate, I'll be all unto you but you have a part to play." Your part is to surrender your life to the Lordship of the Lord Jesus Christ. The question is, "Have you really surrendered?" We carry the emblem on our head that Jesus saves. You tell others that Jesus saves and you pretend to be in a relationship with him. But alas! We are not even sure of your salvation nor are we sure if you have been genuinely saved. Check if you have broken the covenant. A contract is a legal and binding agreement between two or more people. The key word here is "binding". Therefore, when you enter into a contract with God to serve Him, it is binding.

When you enter into a contract for God to protect you, to be your shepherd, you must be ready to be a sheep to Him because that is what makes the contract binding.

Are you really a sheep to Him or a goat? Some Christians make themselves goats not sheep. This is one major reason why God cannot go further with some people. The reason why they struggle is because what God told them to do yesterday, they've not done it; forgetting that with God, if you've not obeyed the last instruction, He would not give you a further instruction.

In Genesis 12, out of so many people in the world, God singled out Abraham (then called Abram) to bless him. God told him that he would be a father of many nations, and that through him the whole universe would be blessed; but one thing he had to do at that junction was to leave his father's house and his kindred, and go to a place that God would show him. If he left his father's house and his kindred, God would do what He said He would do." That became a binding contract. God gave an instruction and waited for that contract to be enacted. A step from Abram would enact it – however, as Abram was leaving, he took Lot, one of the very people that God said he should leave behind. Abram took Lot with him and God refused to talk to Abram because he had not obeyed the last instruction so it was a waste of time for God to give any further instructions.

The reason why some folks are where they are today is because they refused to follow the instruction that God gave them yesterday, so God would not give further instruction until they've acted.

The Bible says that God appeared unto Abram again after Lot had departed. Our churches today are full of broken promises. Church people, the same people who are meant to be the light of the world, who the Bible says that the whole world is waiting for their manifestation; are the same people who when they tell you good morning, you have to check to make sure it is really morning.

How many times have you made promises to your fellow brethren and even to your children and you haven't keep them? My wife once scolded me about this subject matter. One day, I said to my eldest daughter, "If you do well in your exam, you would get a laptop as a gift." The little girl put all her effort into her work and came out brilliantly even more than I had asked for.

Twice my daughter reminded me about my promise and on both occasions I told her I have not forgotten but did not do anything about it. Until one day, my wife preached to me and said; "sweetheart, I think your promise to Debbie is becoming a broken promise"; "You are teaching her bad conduct." She continued. That day, I really felt awful. I realised that I was breaking my promise and decided to change from that day on. If you are like me, please change your attitude.

Think about it, if you can break your promises with someone you can see, what stops you from breaking it with God whom you cannot see? If it's so easy to break our covenant with ourselves e.g. the same young man who says to a lady today, " I love you, you are the butter on my bread, the cream on my coffee, the sugar in my tea - I'll marry you", would run away tomorrow with another lady leaving broken promises behind. If you can break it with your fellow being, do you not think that you'll break it with God that you cannot see? Each time you break a promise with God, you are lengthening the time or the duration you spend in the wilderness because as I've said earlier, God will not give you further instructions until you have obeyed the last one.

I remember when I was working in a Psychiatric hospital in London, UK; one of the patients picked up a knife and started cutting himself. By the time the nurses got to him, there was blood everywhere. After he was treated, he was asked why he cut himself and the young man replied - because he was too fat. If you remain in a particular crossroad of life due to your inconsistencies, disobedience or broken promises, God remains God. As a pastor, I'm tired of seeing people who have potentials and are gifted in diverse ways with the grace of God on their life and a mandate, but are not excelling due to their own carelessness. Their light is not shining neither is their glory radiating. Do you ever ask yourself why? It might be that they've somehow broken their covenant with God.

6. Idolatry

People often think that because they don't have a shrine in their bedroom, nor special room in their houses where they put carved images of gods, and are not pouring oil on this small god, that the problem of idolatry does not apply to them, if you are in that category of people who think this way, I've got news for you; it is not until you have a small god in your pocket (like the one my father gave me in secondary school as protection from anyone who tried to attack me), that you are idolaters. If you want to talk about idolatry, the first thing that comes to your mind is Exodus 32, where the Israelites convinced Aaron to make a golden calf for them which they worshipped.

"You can be sure that no immoral, impure, or greedy person will inherit the Kingdom of Christ and of God. For a greedy person is an idolater, worshiping the things of this world. Don't be fooled by those who try to excuse these sins, for the anger of God will fall on all who disobey him." **- Ephesians 5:5-6**

According to this passage of the Bible, greed equates idolatry. If you are greedy, you are an idol worshipper. I study the Bible using the Living Translation and during my study, I discovered that the Bible calls a greedy person an idolater. What makes a greedy person an idolater? Anything you place value on more than God amounts to idolatry. If you value your job more than God, you are an idolater. If you love your food more than God and your belly is more important to you than God - that is idolatry. I once told our workers during the workers meeting that when God is asking you to fast, and you are saying 'sorry God, not today! I can't fast', even though you know that it is compulsory for workers to fast at least once a week - that is idolatry.

The later part of the above scripture says, *"Do not be deceived or try to excuse these sins, for the anger of God will fall on <u>ALL</u> who disobey him"*. Does that mean that the anger of God would fall on those who are greedy? Yes! You heard well friends. Some people can't stop eating; so your inability to stop eating can invoke the wrath of God. Some people are so greedy that they can't pay their tithe, the percentage that belongs to God of your income (10%);

that is still greed, isn't it? You received seven things from an individual and she asks you back for the smallest of the seven and you say to her, "No! I can't give it to you". "Didn't you just give them to me"? That is called greed. That person is an idolater whose action will surely anger God.

If you check why you were not in church last Sunday and two Sundays ago, you would find out that it might be greed. Could it be that you were not in church because you would be paid triple for working on Sunday? Did you choose extra money over God? You've always known that greed is not good but you have never seen it this way, and for those who have seen it this way, maybe you do not know that its consequence is the wrath of God. Maybe if you did know, you would have changed. Now that you know, do change.

The effect of idolatry; what it can do to a man.

In the book of Exodus 3: 7, 10, the Bible says, *"⁷ Then the Lord told him, "I have certainly seen the oppression of my people in Egypt. I have heard their cries of distress because of their harsh slave drivers. Yes, I am aware of their suffering."*

¹⁰ *Now go, for I am sending you to Pharaoh. You must lead <u>my people</u> Israel out of Egypt."*

Exodus 4: 22 says, *"Then you will tell him, 'this is what the Lord says: Israel is <u>my firstborn son</u>."*

"My people" and "my firstborn son" in this chapter refer to the Israelites but the story changed the day that they made up their mind to become idolaters. The people who were meant to be the people of God decided to make a golden calf and worship it.

Exodus 32: 7-14, the Bible says, *"⁷ The LORD told Moses, "Quick! Go down the mountain! <u>Your people</u> whom you brought from the land of Egypt have corrupted themselves.*

⁸ How quickly they have turned away from the way I commanded them to live! They have melted down gold and made a calf, and they have bowed down and sacrificed to it. They are saying, 'These are your gods, O Israel, who brought you out of the land of Egypt.'"

⁹ Then the LORD said, "I have seen how stubborn and rebellious these people are. ¹⁰ Now leave me alone so my fierce anger can blaze against them, and I will destroy them. Then I will make you, Moses, into a great nation." ¹¹ But Moses tried to pacify the LORD his God. "O LORD!" he said. "Why are you so angry with your own people whom you brought from the land of Egypt with such great power and such a strong hand? ¹² Why let the Egyptians say, 'Their God rescued them with the evil intention of slaughtering them in the mountains and wiping them from the face of the earth'? Turn away from your fierce anger. Change your mind about this terrible disaster you have threatened against your people!

¹³ Remember your servants Abraham, Isaac, and Jacob. You bound yourself with an oath to them, saying, 'I will make your descendants as numerous as the stars of heaven. And I will give them all of this land that I have promised to your descendants, and they will possess it forever.'" ¹⁴ So the LORD changed his mind about the terrible disaster he had threatened to bring on his people."

In the first scripture, God referred to the Israelites as 'my people' but as soon as they became idolaters, God referred to them in a conversation with Moses as 'your people'.

Idolatry will make God change your status and greed will make God disown you. It is so shocking that God said *"your people whom you brought from the land of Egypt have corrupted themselves."* Was it Moses that brought them out of Egypt? No! It was God, He only used Moses.

In verse 9, God said *"I have seen how stubborn and rebellious these people are."* These were the same people who were Gods people and of whom God had said in Exodus 4:22 *"This is what the LORD says: Israel is my firstborn son. I commanded you, "Let my son go..."* I like that story and each time I read it, I liked Moses more. Moses was a shepherd man doing his own thing when God called him and told him to go and deliver His people out of Egypt because He had heard their cry.

Now because they messed up by becoming idolaters, God said that they were no more his people and that they were now Moses people; but Moses replied and said to God, "They are your own people whom you delivered". Now what is the source of this conflict? Idolatry! Idolatry would extend your years in the wilderness. You want to be rich and God wants you to be rich as well, because it is His will that you prosper and be in good health even as your soul prospers according to 3 John 2. One of the reasons why you are not yet as rich might be greed.

Every idolater is disowned by God. May God never disown you! It's a terrible thing for God to disown an individual. Whatever takes priority over God amounts to idolatry even if it is TV, your job, husband, children and wife; it is idolatry. God considers it to be idolatry. Whatever you give value to more than God equates idolatry and God disowns such a person.

7. Rebellion

One of the reasons why the Israelites stayed too long in the wilderness was because of rebellion. They repeatedly rebelled against God and it became a way of life. How many times have you rebelled against God? It takes grace not to rebel against God in a single day. You know the Holy Spirit is a gentle voice, and could be rebelled against for instance, when you are sleeping and God wants to prevent an impending calamity because of his love for you, He says to you, "Daughter, wake up and pray." And your response to him is, "I would pray in the morning", and you go back to sleep.

You think that you are not rebelling because you are not looking at it from a God's perspective. Every time God says bless somebody because the person needs something, and you know it yourself that the Holy Spirit is prompting you to do this and you say, 'not now but maybe during her birthday next year I will do it', you are rebelling. Every disobedience equals rebellion. Rebellion can make God do what he has never done before. Like the story of Korah, Dathan and Abiram who rebelled against a man, not God. They rebelled against Moses (the representative of God) in the book of Numbers 16 and as a result of their rebellion, God commanded the earth to open up and swallow them.

You might think that being rebellious is not your style because whatever God asks of you, you do it. But what about the one God prompted someone to tell you to do? If you don't do it, it is still rebellion. When you hear the word of God through His representative and the Holy Spirit prompting you to take an action but you ignore it that is rebellion. Something that had never happened before happened as a result of this act of rebellion; an earthquake.

God told Moses to tell the people to run away from their camp because anyone around the camp would have been swallowed up by the earth along with the camp of Korah, Dathan and Abiram.

Rebellion does not only affect you, it can also affect the people around you. It can affect your husband, wife, children and your lineage. Then God said to Moses, 'I am angry because these people rebelled against you, so I am about to do what I have never done before, therefore tell them to run away from their camp because my anger is coming and the anger of God came and the earth opened up and swallowed them alive, they were buried alive.' What shocked me most is fact that there was a possibility that when the earth opened up and swallowed them alive, they did not die immediately. Their death would have probably been a gradual thing. First, there would be no oxygen and before they know what was happening, they would have given up. It is possible that before they were swallowed up by the earth they had the chance to ask God for forgiveness but they did not. But as for you, you are still alive today and you have the opportunity to repent. Please do so now!

For some people, when they don't know that something is a sin, there is a possibility that they would run away from it, but as soon as they know it is a sin, they are inclined to run into it. They are being controlled by the spirit of rebellion. There are also some people who come to church and are naturally givers. They give to others but when it comes to giving in the church, they change their countenance; it is rebellion. How many times have you been in church and you hear 'give' and within you is a tumult? You are rebelling!

Naturally, if you had not been asked you could have given ten times the amount asked for but because you have been asked, you refuse to give. You are rebelling for being asked. How many times have you heard that people left the church because they were asked for money? Their spirit rebelled against it, but what they do not know is that maybe what they were meant to give that day was what they needed to do to get out of their wilderness. What they often do is that they move from a church where they are being asked to give and they move to a church where they are not being asked to give, and because their breakthrough is subject to them giving that thing, they stay in that wilderness. The irony of it is that they may not have the opportunity to hear it again and as a result, their trouble continues.

In Mathew 25:1-30, Jesus told us about the "The parable of the talents". In that parable, the servant with only one talent did nothing positive with it except to bury that one talent. He even went to the extent of accusing his master of having the habit of reaping where he has not sown. This is rebellion. The guy was rebelling against the decision of his master forgetting that his master had given him that one talent based on his ability. Anytime you hide the gift of God in your life friends, you are rebelling against Him. And please don't forget that this can prolong your time in the wilderness of life.

CHAPTER 6

Consequences of staying too long in Your Wilderness

To stop cycles of frustrating challenges, you need to know why you shouldn't accept to stay there too long.

Prolonged Trouble

Some people's problems have been prolonged for too long. For some people, it's easy for them to get things done but for some others, when it comes to their turn, it is as if something recognises them and things just change against them. At a certain age in their family, everyone gets married but when it comes to their turn, something just happens. What takes others a day to achieve, takes them a hundred days to achieve. Others are battling with a repeated chain of challenges while their mates move on.

It happened in my life and I would share it with you. I went to a polytechnic before going to do my degree in the university. One day, while I was in the polytechnic, I realised that all my life until then; when it is my turn for something good, something would always happen that would make the good thing elude me. For example, during my primary school, when I was in primary six, the stage where school prefects are chosen, some of my classmates started a riot in the school and the school authority decided to pick the school prefects for that year from the class-set below us (primary five), thus by-passing my class.

When I got to secondary school, I was made a school prefect when we got to class four. While we were still trying to settle down to enjoy the benefits of been made a school prefect, some of the students in my year went and started a riot (I could hear you say "another riot" Yes! Another riot) and our selection was cancelled and all the newly selected prefects were eventually suspended, the school authority was of the opinion that we started the riot. The school went ahead to choose the next set of prefects from class four, a class lower than us as we were already in class five.

Now when I got to the polytechnic, I was already born again and tongue talking. When it was time to elect people into the leadership positions of the then Christian Union, I was made the assistant secretary, even though everyone was expecting me to be made the head of the prayer ministry as I was very active in this ministry and I do oversee the department most of the time when the current leader would be away. All of a sudden, it occurred to me that this had become a prolonged trouble. I immediately remembered my primary school saga and my secondary school episode.

I remembered that when I left secondary school, a man of God prophesised over me that God want to use me but I would need to pray seriously that I will not be short-changed in life. So when I was told that I was being made an assistant secretary, I revolted in my spirit and fervently prayed to Jehovah. There was nothing wrong with being an assistant secretary of the Christian Union, any leadership position at all at that time was highly respected but only I knew my prolonged problem. I fought it in the spirit on my knees and I won the battle. If I had refused to fight that battle in that wilderness, who knows what would have become of me today. For a lot of people, that is the story of their life. When it is their turn for good, things would always go in the opposite direction for them, and it has been like that for years. Friends, let's end this story of my life by saying that my story changed from that day.

For a lot of people, the same battle they have been fighting five years ago, is what they are still battling with today, their prayer point has not changed over the years. Could it be that you have not passed the test in your wilderness by which promotion, advancement and progress would come? If you refuse to learn your wilderness lessons you might as well stay where you are. The prolonged problem you are experiencing might be as a result of staying too long in your wilderness, it is time to move on.

Diseases

If you stay too long in the wilderness, diseases would come. What is a disease? If you separate the word by removing the 'dis' from the rest, what you have left is ease. Therefore, anything that does not give your life ease is a disease; let's ignore the dictionary definition. Disease is the opposite of ease, just as displeased is the opposite of pleased. Anything that does not make life easy for you is a disease. In the Bible, you would find that most of the people that died in the wilderness died of one disease or the other, apart from the three that the earth swallowed. Financial disease, marital disease, academic disease and relationship diseases; do not make life palatable to you. Regarding the Israelites, Exodus 32:35 says, *"And the Lord plagued the people because they worshipped Aaron's calf"*

Termination of Destiny

If you stay too long in the wilderness, your destiny can be terminated and your vision can die. There are people who have a very good vision. For example, God might have told you when you were at a certain age that you are going to be someone special. Mostly, these prophesies are so good that we can't wait for them to happen. Do you know that your life is like a written story to God? If it has been written in the story of someone that he needed to achieve AB squared, he would need to multiply A and B two times, to achieve his purpose, any other formula would not work. The formula for Jesus Christ to inherit a name that is above all names was for him to die a shameful death on the cross, and to resurrect on the third day. If Jesus had refused to submit himself to be crucified, there could not be a death and resurrection.

Even when He tried to see if the formula could be changed, he immediately realised, that is the only winning formula. The earlier He agreed to the formula of God the sooner He would get out of the wilderness. God has made some to see the formula of their lives, and God made them to realise what they need to do to get to their Promised Land and yet some people refuse to do it.

The more a man stays in the wilderness, the more chances are that his destiny might be terminated.

People's destinies and visions have collapsed and died because they refused to yield to God's instruction. That instruction might be from God to you, it might be through a man of God to you, or it might be through situations that God is using to propel you towards that time. Each time you resist, you delay the performance of God's vision for your life.

Isn't it amazing that as close as Moses was to God; he saw the back of God - yet after he came from the presence of God, he was so radiant that people could not behold his face and he had to cover his face with a veil so that people could speak to him.

He was that close to God and yet he had his destiny terminated due to the fact that his old weakness -anger- showed up again because he had stayed too long in the wilderness. If they had crossed over into the Promised Land on the 48th day, there wouldn't be any need for water to come out of the rock and Moses would not have struck the rock when God told him to speak to the rock but because they did not cross over on the 48th day, his destiny was altered.

The success of yesterday does not guarantee the success of today.

Some people like it so much in the wilderness that they don't want to get out. They easily forget that there are wild beasts in the wilderness. Wild beasts can rupture your faith, wild beasts can destroy your standing with God, and wild beasts can prevent you from entering the Promised Land which is the destination. The wilderness is just a bus stop and not a bus terminal; there is a big difference between the two. Some people get to the bus stop of their lives and camp there, when God is saying, "My son, and my daughter! All I am expecting you to do is just to stop for one or two seconds and move on." Instead, they put up their tent there forgetting that grace for the wilderness can expire.

When the grace for the wilderness expires, struggle steps in, struggle leads to frustration, which leads to doubt, doubt will lead to unbelief which leads to compromise, compromise leads to failure, and perpetual failure will eventually lead to termination of destiny.

The grace for your current position may have expired and some of you may be living on expired grace –That wilderness time should be up by now.

Discouragement

"And they journeyed from Mount Hor by the way to the Red Sea, to go around the land of Edom, and the people became impatient (depressed, much discouraged), because [of the trials] of the way." - **Numbers 21:4 (Amplified)**

Norman Vincent Pearle said, "The secret of life isn't what happened to you, it is what you do with what happened to you."

Discouragement always shows up when you stay too long in the wilderness. Discouragement is a spiritual killer. It weakens or depresses the heart, causes heaviness, brings disappointment, discontentment, loss of confidence in oneself, loss of enthusiasm, emotional breakdown and the motivation to keep going on. The Israelites lost their zeal, their enthusiasm and their interest to continue on their journey due to the challenges and problems they encountered on their way to the Promised Land. They became discouraged to the point that their soul was affected and once the soul of a man is affected, the totality of his well-being will be affected. Many have allowed this spirit of discouragement to destroy the plans and purposes of God for their lives. Some people have committed suicide as a result of discouragement.

The path to success is not a rosy one. Even in our walk with God, disappointment would surface from time to time but how you deal with it is what differentiates you from others. David was greatly distressed, for the men spoke of stoning him because their souls were bitterly grieved, each man for his sons and daughters. But David encouraged and strengthened himself in the Lord his God (1 Samuel 30:6). When discouragement sets in, all you need to do is encourage yourself with the WORD OF GOD.

Unfulfilled Vision

[7] "The LORD said to Moses, [8] "Take the staff, and you and your brother Aaron gather the assembly together. Speak to that rock before their eyes and it will pour out its water. You will bring water out of the rock for the community so they and their livestock can drink." [9] So Moses took the staff from the LORD's presence, just as he commanded him. [10] He and Aaron gathered the assembly together in front of the rock and Moses said to them, "Listen, you rebels, must we bring you water out of this rock?" [11] Then Moses raised his arm and struck the rock twice with his staff. Water gushed out, and the community and their livestock drank. [12] But the LORD said to Moses and Aaron, "Because you did not trust in me enough to honour me as holy in the sight of the Israelites, you will not bring this community into the land I give them." - **Numbers 20: 7-12**

Vision is not fulfilled in the wilderness; it is fulfilled in the Promised Land. God instructed Moses to speak to the rock but instead Moses smote the rock twice. He allowed his anger against the people to get the worst out of him, he wanted to take the glory for himself, he did not honour God in the sight of the people as a result he was not given the opportunity to lead the people to the Promised Land as promised by God.

"Since you did not have faith in Me to sanctify Me in the eyes of the children of Israel, therefore you shall not bring this assembly to the Land which I have given them." - **Numbers 20:12**

God is no respecter of persons. It doesn't matter who you are once God has given you a command, you must follow it to the letter for your vision to be realised. You must fear God rather than man. Disobedience, taking the glory for oneself and not honouring God would terminate one's vision in the wilderness.

Inability to Possess What You See
"Aaron will be gathered to his people. He will not enter the land I give the Israelites, because both of you rebelled against my command at the waters of Meribah." - **Numbers 20:24**

The spirit of almost-there-but-never-there can stop you from possessing what you see. When you stay too long in the wilderness of life, you would only see and not touch. Moses and Aaron only saw the promise but did not enjoy the blessing because they were cut up in a supposed short journey that turned long. The unordained duration of the journey made Moses' weakness raises its head one more time. Consequently, he was able to see physically the much-awaited Promised Land (unlike Abraham who saw spiritually with the power of his imagination) and yet he did not possess it.

As for Aaron, despite the fact that he did very well to support Moses at the beginning of the journey to the Promised Land, the unanticipated long journey made him doubt Moses like the others and he inevitably suffered the consequence. Doubt is a sin like the sin of rebellion. How many times has God shown you that vision or promise and yet you doubted him? God has sent some people your way to ascertain the promises, yet because the problem is prolonged you doubted or discredited the word of God. James 1: 6-7 says, **"But when you ask, you must believe and not doubt, because the one who doubts is like a wave of the sea, blown and tossed by the wind. ⁷ That person should not expect to receive anything from the Lord."** Once you doubt God or His word, it changes everything.

Death
"When the Canaanite king of Arad, who lived in the Negev, heard that Israel was coming along the road to Atharim, he attacked the Israelites and captured some of them. ² Then Israel made this vow to the LORD: "If you will deliver these

*people into our hands, we will totally destroy their cities."
³The LORD listened to Israel's plea and gave the Canaanites
over to them. They completely destroyed them and their
towns; so the place was named Hormah. ⁴ They travelled
from Mount Hor along the route to the Red Sea, to go around
Edom. But the people grew impatient on the way; ⁵ they spoke
against God and against Moses, and said, "Why have you
brought us up out of Egypt to die in the wilderness? There
is no bread! There is no water! And we detest this miserable
food!" ⁶ Then the LORD sent venomous snakes among them;
they bit the people and many Israelites died. ⁷The people
came to Moses and said, "We sinned when we spoke against
the LORD and against you. Pray that the LORD will take
the snakes away from us." So Moses prayed for the people."*
- Numbers 21:1-7

The wages or the penalty of sin is death. From the above
passage, the children of Israel sinned by speaking against God
and against Moses because they were going through a time
of difficulty. Moses himself was not left out of the resulting
death due to his own failings. The more they remained in
the wilderness, the more likely it was that they would not
complete the journey. One of the sins that brought death upon
the Israelites was complaining and murmuring.

Pause for a minute and think, what has complaining and
murmuring done for you? It has only brought death. Yes death!
It might not be physical death but death in your spiritual life,
business, marriage, career, ministry, finances, etc. In what
area are you in the wilderness? Is it in your walk with God,
your ministry, your calling, your career, your business, your
relationships or marriage, your finances? Is it in the actualisation
of your vision or the purpose of God for your life? Is it in
finding fulfilment whether of prophesy or dream; remember it
is a necessity that you must pass through the wilderness to get

to your Promised Land. Wilderness is a bus stop and not a bus terminal. Everyone who permanently or perpetually remains in the wilderness will eventually die there. May you never die in your wilderness in Jesus name, Amen!

CHAPTER 7

Timing is Important to Every Achievement

E verything that has a manufacture date also has an expiry date. Even in countries where manufacture and expiry dates are not being attended to closely, things are changing. That's why we have NAFDAC in my home country (Nigeria) to make sure that this crucial practice becomes very important. There must be a manufacture and expiry date for consumable products. Most of the things that we are going through now are already expired spiritually, and some Christians are going through problems and challenges that are already expired.

The beauty of an achievement relates to the timing of that achievement.

We need to know that life and all it entails is timed. If God wants you to be in the wilderness for two days and you are spending five years there, that is not God's problem. God would not change his law because of you; you are the one who needs to change to fit into the laws of God, therefore, if God is leading you into a wilderness and God expects you to spend three hours in that wilderness and five years later you are still in that wilderness, even if you come out of that wilderness, there is no more beauty in that achievement.

A 120-year old man who has no teeth in his mouth and has got dementia was told about the lottery and he sent for his grandson to buy him a lottery ticket. The grandson bought the ticket and the old man won £10 million pounds. His sons could not inform him about his big win. If they do, he could have a heart attack and die. If per chance God saved him and he did not die, is winning a lottery at 120 years old a good achievement for a man who can't even chew his food anymore? No! The reason why it is not a good achievement is that firstly, he can die tomorrow; secondly, the better part of his life is gone. Although you can say a good man leaves an inheritance for his children's children, what is the probability that if he leaves that inheritance for his sons who did not work for it, that they would not spoil everything in one day? That is not a good achievement because the beauty of an achievement relates to the time of that achievement.

The time that you spend in the wilderness is subject to you because you are the determining factor. Please don't allow a journey that is meant for two years to go on for ten years because it would lose its beauty after grace has expired. Maybe you once saw someone caring for somebody and you decided that you want to become a nurse and you go through all the wilderness of the course and you refused to let the wild beast of the course and the project disturb you, and you came out with your nursing qualification and you are a nurse today. What made you a nurse today? Your decision of yesterday!

I once read of a man who at the age of ninety decided to go back to the university and he spent five years in the university and graduated with first class honours, which is a very good achievement for a ninety year old man. During his graduation, he was separated to be honoured specially. That is a bad honour because what was he doing when he was 20, 25 or 30 years old? Your certificate is not for show off. When you spend so much money to go to the university and you get your certificate, it is meant to help make your life better. Who is going to employ a 95 years old man? Nobody! That is not a good achievement. Don't let the journey of 10 days become 10 years in your hand because it's not worth it. How long you stay in your wilderness is subject to your obedience, your conformity and your adaptability to the instructions and the word of God. Make a good choice today knowing that your choice in life determines your chance in life. You are today the product of the choices you made yesterday.

Your choice in life determines your chance in life; so please make a choice today not to allow the journey of 10 days become 10 years in your hands. Allow yourself to be trained because if you are not teachable then you are not reachable.

God bless

About the Author

Idris Kolade Oyinlade is the senior pastor of RCCG City of David, Cambridge. He is a trained accountant now in full-time ministry with a vision to help people find and fulfil their God-given purpose in life.

Oyinlade is a teacher of the word of faith and enjoys the grace of God as an apostle. He preaches the gospel with passion and has travelled extensively around Europe, the United States, and Africa, impacting lives.

He is married to Olayinka Oyinlade, and they are blessed with three prophetic children: Deborah, Isaac, and Shalom.

Contact the Author
Idris Kolade Oyinlade

Rccg City of David Cambridge Unit BC The Paddocks
347 Cherry Hinton Road Cambridge CB1 8DH
Phone numbers: +441223415417,+447984936120

pastorkolade@rccgcambridge.org.uk http://
www.rccgcambridge.org.uk

Lightning Source UK Ltd.
Milton Keynes UK
UKOW02f0402090716

277987UK00001B/38/P